Get More From
The TI99/4A

Get More From The TI99/4A

Garry Marshall

GRANADA
London Toronto Sydney New York

Granada Technical Books
Granada Publishing Ltd
8 Grafton Street, London W1X 3LA

First published in Great Britain by
Granada Publishing 1983

British Library Cataloguing in Publication Data
Marshall, Garry
    Get more from the TI99/4A.
    1. Texas   TI99/4A (Computer)
    I. Title
    001.64'04   QA76.8.T/

ISBN 0-246-12281-1

Typeset by V & M Graphics Ltd, Aylesbury, Bucks
Printed and bound in Great Britain

Contents

Preface

This book is about getting more from the Texas Instruments TI99/4A computer. The way of doing this that it advocates is to learn to program the TI99/4A effectively. Now, the User's Reference Guide that is supplied with the computer gives a rather good treatment of the features of TI BASIC and makes an excellent source of reference. It is not so good at explaining how to write and develop programs, however. This book aims to supplement the User's Reference Guide by showing how to develop interesting programs. By the same token, it avoids repeating material from the Guide, except for a little of the introductory material that must be included to make the book self-contained.

After a broad introduction to the features of TI BASIC in Chapter 1, the book moves on to developing short programs for colour graphics and sound effects in Chapter 2. In Chapter 3, it concentrates more on graphics and the production of effective screen displays. In the second and third chapters most of the features of TI BASIC that are needed in later chapters are introduced. At the same time utility routines are developed for performing tasks that cannot be achieved directly in TI BASIC. Chapter 4 provides a discussion on how to develop lengthy programs in a systematic way and on how to document them to make them readable. Then Chapters 5 to 8 are devoted to the development of some fairly long programs for interesting applications, including a Space Invader game and a simulation. All the programs presented in these chapters are written to take advantage of the particular strengths of the TI99/4A. The final chapter examines how the computer can be expanded, with particular emphasis on the programming languages that are available as alternatives to TI BASIC. In fact, the computer can be expanded with an impressive array of programs and peripherals.

The book does not cover every aspect of TI BASIC. It does,

however, try to provide some motivation for each of the topics that it does cover. I hope that this approach will encourage the reader to use the TI99/4A with confidence, to experiment with its capabilities and, above all, to enjoy using it.

Finally, I should like to thank Richard Miles of Granada Publishing for his continual encouragement and for arranging for me to have the use of a TI99/4A with many programs and peripherals prior to and during the writing of this book. I would also like to thank Texas Instruments for making a TI99/4A available for me.

Garry Marshall

Chapter One
Introduction To TI BASIC

The version of BASIC that is built into the Texas Instruments
TI99/4A is known as TI BASIC. It can always be accessed by
pressing the 1 key when the computer's master selection list is
displayed. Programming the computer in TI BASIC is one way to
get it to do exactly what you want it to do. Whether you want it to
display brilliant colour graphics, to play music, to play a game or to
store and manipulate information, you can make it perform to your
wishes by programming it.

The purpose of this introductory chapter is to introduce the
features of TI BASIC so that we can see what capabilities it
possesses and how they can be used as the building blocks for
constructing programs. Later, in Chapters 2 and 3, we shall write
some quite short programs and, in Chapters 6 to 8, we shall have
progressed to the stage of developing substantial ones. Before
proceeding to write programs of any length however, we shall pause
in Chapter 4 to consider how they can be developed in a systematic
way. Adopting a systematic approach to program development not
only makes it possible for the reader to get the most from the
programs themselves but also helps to ensure that the programs
work properly!

The programs that are presented are intended to do more than
demonstrate how to program the computer. They are all written
with an eye to showing off the capabilities of the TI99/4A. Thus, its
colour graphics and sound production capabilities are prominently
featured. The programs also illustrate the kinds of uses to which
computers can be put. In this way they should provide the reader
with a fund of ideas for what to do with the computer either by
enhancing the programs presented in the book or by using them as a
launching pad for further, personal, developments.

The TI BASIC environment

TI BASIC provides a number of commands that make it easy to use. They are typed in directly and are obeyed as soon as the ENTER key is pressed. Tasks typical of those for which commands are provided are the entering, examining and altering of programs. The following Table 1.1 lists the more useful commands and gives summaries of their purposes.

Table 1.1. Some of the commands of TI BASIC.

Command	Purpose of command
BYE	To leave TI BASIC and return to the master title screen.
EDIT	To edit existing program lines. By typing EDIT followed by a line number, the program line with that number can be amended by replacing, inserting or deleting characters.
LIST	To list the program currently stored in the computer. A part of a program can also be listed by giving the line numbers of the first and last lines in the part as, for example, in LIST 200–300.
NEW	To erase the program currently stored in the computer and to prepare it generally for the entry of a new program.
NUMBER	To generate the line numbers for program lines automatically. When issued by itself the line numbers start at 100 and increase in steps of 10. However, the command can specify the starting number and the step as in NUMBER 200, 50 which gives an initial line number of 200 and then the numbers 250, 300 and so on.
OLD	To copy a program that is stored on cassette, or some other permanent storage medium, into the computer's memory. The command causes the instructions for operating the cassette recorder to be generated and displayed automatically.
RUN	To run the program that is currently stored in the computer.
SAVE	To save the program that is currently stored in the computer by copying it onto cassette or some other permanent storage medium. As with OLD, the instructions for operating the cassette recorder are generated and displayed automatically.

The features of TI BASIC

In essence, what most computer programs do is to accept and store information, to manipulate the information in some way, and to present the results of this to the person using the program. This pattern is evident in an arcade game program such as Space Invaders where the person playing the game provides the inputs by pressing keys as are appropriate for moving his missile base and for firing missiles. The inputs are manipulated by, first, determining which command they represent and then taking the appropriate action such as moving the missile launcher to the left. The result of this is presented to the user by an appropriate modification to the display screen. As an example from the use of computers in business, a stock control program gives a direct reflection of the pattern. Changes in stock are typically provided to the stock control program as inputs. This information is manipulated so that a correct representation of the current stock position is stored in the computer, and this can be displayed to show the state of the stock at any time. When a computer runs a program to enable it to control another item of electronic equipment, the program accepts as input signals from the equipment it is controlling. It then processes these signals to determine what action it needs to take, and then produces as output the control signals that will cause the necessary actions to be taken. Since most computer programs conform to this pattern, all computer languages, and TI BASIC in particular, must have features with which a programmer can direct the computer to accept information, store it, manipulate it, and display the results. Some of these actions can be achieved with commands, and we shall demonstrate this before moving on to show them being done by simple programs.

We can store a word such as 'Houston' in the memory of the computer by making an *assignment*. This is done by enclosing the word in quotation marks and assigning it to a variable. To do this we must give the name of the variable. A variable name should begin with a letter, it can be from one to fifteen characters long, and the other characters can be letters or numbers. (Actually, a few other characters can be placed at the beginning of or within a variable name, but we shall not do so in this book.) As far as possible, variables will be given names in this book which indicate the purpose to which they are being put. This helps to make programs more readable and easy to understand. Finally, if a word, rather than a number, is to be assigned to a variable, then the name of the variable must end with a dollar sign. This is so the computer can tell when it is dealing with words and when it is handling numbers. Thus, one way to store our word is with the assignment command:

CITY$ = "HOUSTON"

When it is executed it causes the string of seven characters in the word to be stored in a part of the computer's memory which can be referred to as CITY$.

Numbers can be stored using similar assignments. For example, we can store the numbers five and six with the two assignments:

FIVE = 5
SIX = 6

Again, these numbers are stored in parts of the computer's memory that can be referenced by the names of the respective variables to which they are assigned.

With two numbers stored in the computer, we can write commands which cause these numbers to be processed and to store the results. For example, we can find and store the sum and the difference of the two numbers with

SUM = SIX + FIVE

and

DIFFERENCE = SIX − FIVE

When one of these commands is executed what happens is that the computer takes the part of the command to the right of the equals sign, which is written as it would be in ordinary arithmetic, and uses it to find a value. Thus, when finding the sum, it looks up the values assigned to the variables FIVE and SIX, and adds these values together. When a value has been found as a result of dealing with the right-hand side of an assignment, it is assigned to the variable whose name is given on the left-hand side. So, when the last two commands have been executed we have 11 stored under SUM and one stored under DIFFERENCE.

When these commands are obeyed there is no external evidence that anything has occurred, since they have caused events to happen only inside the computer, in its memory. However, to find out what has happened there we can use the PRINT command or, to equal effect, the DISPLAY command. Either of the commands

PRINT CITY$

and

DISPLAY CITY$

will cause whatever is stored under the variable name CITY$ to be displayed on the screen. In this case we shall see

HOUSTON

To see what is stored in the variables FIVE and SIX and the results that were stored in SUM and DIFFERENCE we can give the command

PRINT FIVE, SIX, SUM, DIFFERENCE

or

DISPLAY FIVE, SIX, SUM, DIFFERENCE

They will both cause the display

```
    5        6
    11       1
```

In this way, with simple assignment commands and commands involving PRINT or DISPLAY we can cause the computer to store and manipulate information, and to display the results. Each command is obeyed at once, and so to achieve a chain of actions we have to enter the successive commands one after another following the completion of the prior commands.

We turn now to writing programs to tell the computer what to do, rather than giving it commands to do one thing at a time. A *program* is a sequence of instructions that tells the computer how to perform a task when the sequence is obeyed. The computer must *store* the program first. When it is stored completely, it can be run using the RUN command. When a command is preceded by a number the computer recognises it as a program line and proceeds to store it as part of the current program. The number is usually referred to as a *line number* and the combination of number and command as a *program line* or *statement*. The computer uses the line numbers to order the program lines, constructing a program by placing the lines in increasing order of their line numbers.

A simple program to store two numbers, find their sum and difference, and display the result can be written based on previously given commands.

It is

```
100 FIVE = 5
110 SIX = 6
120 SUM = SIX + FIVE
130 DIFFERENCE = SIX - FIVE
140 DISPLAY FIVE, SIX, SUM, DIFFERENCE
150 END
```

Remember that just typing in the program as it is written automatically causes it to be stored. It can be listed by issuing the LIST command and run as often as you like by issuing the RUN command repeatedly.

This program is of strictly limited value since it always finds the sum and difference of the same two numbers. We can generalise it so that it can do the same for any two numbers that we might care to give the program when it is running by using the INPUT statement. When an INPUT statement is executed it causes the computer to display a question mark as a prompt and then to wait until an entry is typed and ENTER is pressed, when it assigns the entered value to the variable mentioned in the statement. Thus, execution of the statement

```
100 INPUT FIVE
```

will cause the entered value to be assigned to the variable named FIVE. The facility also exists for providing your own prompt rather than the question mark, and well-designed prompts make a program much easier to use. If we would like the prompt

```
FIRST NUMBER?
```

to appear when we should enter the first number, we can write the INPUT statement as

```
100 INPUT "FIRST NUMBER?" : FIVE
```

Note the use of the colon, which is compulsory. A program to accept any two numbers and find their sum and difference can now be written as:

```
100 INPUT "FIRST NUMBER?" : NUMBER1
110 INPUT "SECOND NUMBER?" : NUMBER2
120 SUM = NUMBER1 + NUMBER2
130 DIFFERENCE = NUMBER1 - NUMBER2
140 DISPLAY NUMBER1,NUMBER2, SUM, DIFFERENCE
150 END
```

A typical dialogue produced by running this program is:

```
FIRST NUMBER? 10
SECOND NUMBER? 2
10        2
12        8
```

Another way of providing data to a program is to use the READ and DATA statements. With these, the data (whether numbers or words) is given in the DATA statement or statements. The first READ statement that is executed in a program causes the first item of data to be read, the second READ statement reads the second item and so on. Clearly, since the data items must be explicitly listed in a DATA statement they must be known at the time the program is written. If this is not the case, then the use of an INPUT statement is probably a more appropriate way of providing data. The use of the READ and DATA statements is illustrated by the next program.

```
100 I = 1
110 READ WORD$
120 DISPLAY "WORD NUMBER "; I;" IS "; WORD$
130 I = I + 1
140 GOTO 110
150 DATA ABILENE, GALVESTON, LAREDO, AUSTIN
160 END
```

Note that since the data consists of words it is read into an appropriately named variable, WORD$. The GOTO statement is introduced in line 140. The effect of executing

```
GOTO 110
```

is to cause line 110 to be executed next. When this program is run it produces the display

```
WORD NUMBER 1 IS ABILENE
WORD NUMBER 2 IS GALVESTON
WORD NUMBER 3 IS LAREDO
WORD NUMBER 4 IS AUSTIN
```

```
*DATA ERROR IN 110
```

The program reads and displays the items of data, but it also gives an error. What has happened is that the GOTO statement in line 140 has created a loop that is executed for ever (unless an error occurs). Every time line 140 is reached it sends the computer back to do line 110 again. However, the fifth time that the READ statement in line

110 is executed there is no data to read, for the DATA statement contains only four items. This is the cause of the error.

One way to amend the program is with the use of the *conditional* statement. This has the form:

IF condition THEN line number 1 ELSE line number 2

When executed, the condition is tested. If it is found to be true then the statement having its line number given by line number 1 is done next, otherwise that with the line number given by line number 2 is done next. The statement can be abbreviated to

IF condition THEN line number 1

In this form, the condition is tested, and if it is true the statement with the line number given by line number 1 is done next, otherwise the next line after the conditional statement is executed.

The last program can be corrected if we include a special item of data to indicate that it is the last item, and then use the conditional statement to detect it and cause the program to end properly. The resulting program is:

```
100 I = 1
110 READ WORD$
120 IF WORD$ = "END" THEN 170 ELSE 130
130 DISPLAY "WORD NUMBER "; I;" IS "; WORD$
140 I = I + 1
150 GOTO 110
160 DATA ABILENE, GALVESTON, LAREDO, AUSTIN,
    END
170 END
```

The program will display only the first four data items and not the last one which is only an end-marker and presumably not an item of data as such for the program.

Since the program that gave the error is about reading and displaying a word repeatedly, it could equally well be fixed using TI BASIC's facility for repetition. This involves the use of the FOR and NEXT statements. Using them, an alternative version of the fixed program is:

```
100 FOR I = 1 TO 4
110 READ WORD$
120 DISPLAY "WORD NUMBER "; I;" IS "; WORD$
130 NEXT I
```

140 DATA ABILENE, GALVESTON, LAREDO, AUSTIN
150 END

The repetitions are achieved by repeating the statements between the FOR and NEXT statements as often as directed by the FOR statement. In this case the first repetition is done with $I = 1$, the next with I increased by one to two, the next with I increased by one to three and finally with $I = 4$. The general form of the FOR statement is:

FOR variable = initial value TO final value STEP step

This gives the initial value to be assigned to the variable for the first repetition, the final value for the last repetition and the step by which the initial value is to be increased up to the final value for the repetitions in between. If STEP is omitted, as it is in the last program, it is taken to be one.

Finally, we will introduce TI BASIC's CALL KEY statement. It has the form:

CALL KEY (0, CODE, STATUS)

Its purpose is to allow interactive entry of data to a program. With its use a program can determine whether a key has been pressed and, if so, which one. However, the program does not halt, as it does with an INPUT statement, but proceeds immediately after executing CALL KEY to the next statement as it would with any other statement. When it has been executed, the value of STATUS indicates whether or not a key has been pressed, and the value of CODE gives the code for the character on the key that has been pressed. The codes are explained in full in the next chapter.

Summary

This chapter provided an introduction to the facilities of TI BASIC. First the commands it provides were described. Then the ways in which data entry, storage, manipulation and display can be achieved were explained. Input can be achieved with the INPUT, CALL KEY, and READ and DATA statements. Assignments permit both storage and manipulation. The PRINT and DISPLAY statements can both be used to display results.

Chapter Two
Graphics And Sound

The strong points of the Texas computer include its graphics and sound capabilities, and the ease with which graphics and sound effects can be programmed. In this chapter we shall examine the fundamental techniques for producing graphics displays and for generating sounds.

Graphics

A program or text appears on the screen when letters and numbers are positioned in the appropriate places. Letters and numbers are represented when stored in the computer by their codes. To give one example, the code for 'A' is 65. In fact, the computer uses the ASCII code to represent the standard characters that can be entered from the keyboard. The code is listed in Appendix 1. When the computer is switched on the codes from 32 to 127 are automatically assigned to the characters as shown there.

In the same way as positioning letters on the screen gives a paragraph of text, so a picture can be displayed by placing graphics characters on the screen. To illustrate this, the image shown in Figure 2.1 can be formed by combining the small number of graphics characters in Figure 2.2 in the way illustrated by Figure 2.3.

The computer itself does not provide any graphics characters. However, it does provide the user with the capability to define his own graphics characters. The codes from 128 to 159 have no characters assigned to them, and they are there, in essence, for the user to assign his own characters. Besides this, characters may be reassigned to any of the codes from 32 to 127 within a program if this should suit the user.

Every character that can be displayed on the screen occupies an area that consists of eight rows each with eight dots along it called a

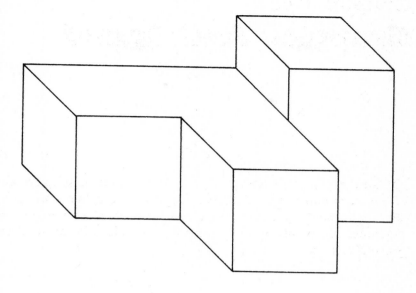

Fig. 2.1. An image.

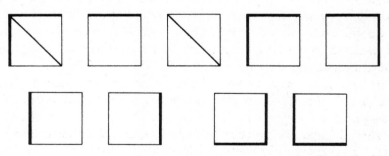

Fig. 2.2. Some graphics characters.

dot matrix. This is equally true whether the machine defines the character automatically or you define it yourself. A character is displayed in this area by (in monochrome terms) turning some of the dots on and leaving others off. Expressing this rather more appropriately in terms of colour, a character is displayed in colour by making some of the dots one colour and the rest another colour.

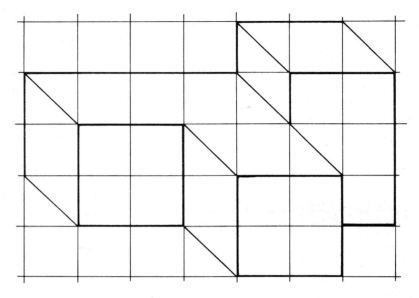

Fig. 2.3. The image of Fig. 2.1 composed of graphics characters.

Thus, the character '5' is produced as shown in Figure 2.4(a) while the first of the graphics characters in Figure 2.2 can be produced as in Figure 2.4(b).

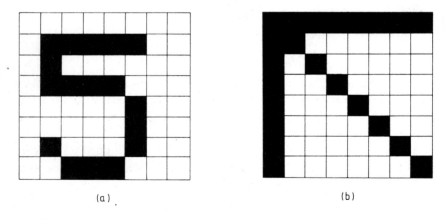

(a)   (b)

Fig. 2.4. (a) Dot matrix for '5'. (b) Dot matrix for a graphics character.

Suppose that we want to use the character shown in Figure 2.4(b) in one of our programs. It can be defined and assigned a code by using the CALL CHAR statement which takes the following form:

CALL CHAR (code, character description)

The character description is arrived at by representing each dot that is on with a 1 and each that is off by a 0, and writing the 0's and 1's down in the same pattern as the dots that make up the character. The string of eight binary digits representing each row is then converted to two hexadecimal digits (see Appendix 2 for an explanation of binary and hexadecimal notation). The whole process is illustrated in Figure 2.5. The character can then be assigned the code 128 by:

CALL CHAR (128, "FFC0A09088848281")

	Binary	Hexadecimal
	11111111	FF
	11000000	C0
	10100000	A0
	10010000	90
	10001000	88
	10000100	84
	10000010	82
	10000001	81

Fig. 2.5. A character and its description.

When a character has been defined in this way in a program it can be plotted on the screen. It can be positioned in any of the 32 columns along any of the 24 rows on the screen. The plotting is done using either of the statements CALL HCHAR or CALL VCHAR. With both of these, a character can be plotted at a specified screen position by giving the row and column of the position to be occupied and the code for the character. The forms of the statements are:

CALL HCHAR (ROW, COLUMN, CODE)

and

CALL VCHAR (ROW, COLUMN, CODE)

Additionally, a character can also be plotted repeatedly along a row (that is, horizontally) using HCHAR and along a column (vertically) with VCHAR. The repetitions start from the specified position and are achieved by placing the number of repetitions after the code in HCHAR and VCHAR.

On the screen, the rows are numbered 1 to 24 from top to bottom, and the columns 1 to 32 from left to right. A short program to define a character and place it in the centre on the screen is:

```
100    CALL CLEAR
110    CALL CHAR(128, "FFC0A09088848281")
120    CALL HCHAR(12, 16, 128)
130    GOTO 130
```

The first line of the program is the CALL CLEAR statement which causes the screen to be cleared when it is executed. The final statement prevents the program from halting so that no messages or prompts can appear to interfere with the display that we are trying to create. The program can be stopped by pressing FCTN 4, the CLEAR key. The third line of the program could equally well be:

120 CALL VCHAR (12, 16, 128)

We can create a border around the screen by placing the solid block character, in which all the dots are turned on, around the edges of the screen with the following program:

```
100    CALL CLEAR
110    CALL CHAR(129, "FFFFFFFFFFFFFFFF")
120    CALL. HCHAR(1, 1, 129, 32)
130    CALL HCHAR(24, 1, 129, 32)
140    CALL VCHAR(1, 1, 129, 24)
150    CALL VCHAR(1, 32, 129, 24)
160    GOTO 160
```

The screen can be completely filled with the same character by:

```
100    CALL CLEAR
110    CALL CHAR(129, "FFFFFFFFFFFFFFFF")
120    FOR ROW=1 TO 24
130    FOR COLUMN=1 TO 32
140    CALL HCHAR(ROW, COLUMN, 129)
150    NEXT COLUMN
160    NEXT ROW
170    GOTO 170
```

However, it can be done much more simply by replacing lines 120 to 160 with either:

120 CALL HCHAR (1, 1, 129, 24*32)

or

120 CALL VCHAR (1, 1, 129, 24*32)

Colour

Colour displays can be created with the use of fifteen colours. The colours are coded from 1 to 16 and are listed with their codes in the following Table 2.1.

Table 2.1. The available colours and their codes.

Colour	Code
Transparent	1
Black	2
Medium green	3
Light green	4
Dark blue	5
Light blue	6
Dark red	7
Cyan	8
Medium red	9
Light red	10
Dark Yellow	11
Light yellow	12
Dark green	13
Magenta	14
Grey	15
White	16

The screen can be set to any of these colours using the CALL SCREEN statement with the code for the required colour. Thus,

CALL SCREEN (5)

sets the screen to dark blue. In the absence of any command to the contrary, the screen becomes light green when a program is running.

When the screen colour is set, we can place characters on it which have their own colours. Any character can be given its own foreground colour for the dots that are on and a background colour for the ones that are off. These colours are assigned using the CALL COLOR statement. For use with COLOR, the range of character codes is divided into sets, each of which contains eight codes. The sets are given in the following Table 2.2, which is repeated for reference in Appendix 1.

Table 2.2. Division of the character codes into sets.

Set number	Codes in set
1	32 – 39
2	40 – 47
3	48 – 55
4	56 – 63
5	64 – 71
6	72 – 79
7	80 – 87
8	88 – 95
9	96 – 103
10	104 – 111
11	112 – 119
12	120 – 127
13	128 – 135
14	136 – 143
15	144 – 151
16	152 – 159

When the CALL COLOR statement is used it assigns foreground and background colours for every character with its code in a particular set. The form of the statement is

CALL COLOR (set, foreground colour, background colour)

and, as an example,

CALL COLOR (13, 6, 5)

assigns to all the characters with codes in set 13, that is those with codes 128 to 135, a foreground colour of light blue and a background colour of dark blue. When colour code 1 is used for either foreground or background colour the screen colour shows through. Until colours are assigned the standard foreground colour is black (code 2) and the background is transparent (code 1).

To illustrate the way in which a coloured display may be produced, consider how we might plot a coloured display consisting of a single line in each of light red, white and dark blue on a cyan screen. Basically, we can do this by plotting on a screen of cyan characters with a cyan background. (We could equally well make the background transparent.) The lines can be made up by using a graphics character with a single horizontal line across it. This character, however, must be used to produce three differently coloured lines. To do this, we use the same character description to define three characters with codes in different sets. We can then assign a different foreground colour to each version of the character. The program to generate our display is:

```
100    CALL CLEAR
110    CALL SCREEN(8)
120    A$="000000FF"
130    CALL CHAR(128, A$)
140    CALL CHAR(136, A$)
150    CALL CHAR(144, A$)
160    CALL COLOR(13,10,8)
170    CALL COLOR(14,16,8)
180    CALL COLOR(15,5,8)
190    CALL HCHAR(4, 1, 128, 32)
200    CALL HCHAR(12, 1, 136, 32)
210    CALL HCHAR(20, 1, 144, 32)
220    GOTO 220
```

As this program suggests, all fifteen colours can appear on the screen simultaneously. Also, characters that are invisible can be placed on the screen. This can be done by making both foreground and background colours of the character transparent. It can be done equally well by making the foreground and background colours the same as the screen colour. A character plotted invisibly in this way can be made visible by changing the colours assigned to it.

Creating large images

Although a tremendous variety of graphics characters can be defined on the eight by eight dot matrix assigned for each character, it is not always possible to design a convincing representation of a fairly complex object on a single character. To illustrate this, an attempt at designing a tank as a single character is shown in Figure 2.6(a). The effectiveness of this design is left for the reader to judge, but it cannot compare with that which can be obtained by using a block of four characters as shown in Figure 2.6(b). The latter tank can be plotted at the centre of the screen with the next program.

```
100    CALL CLEAR
110    CALL CHAR(136, "0000060F1F3F3F1F")
120    CALL CHAR(137, "0000000080FFC0C0")
130    CALL CHAR(138, "073F55BF6A1F")
140    CALL CHAR(139, "80FC57FAACF8")
150    CALL HCHAR(12, 16, 136)
```

```
160    CALL HCHAR(12, 17, 137)
170    CALL HCHAR(13, 16, 138)
180    CALL HCHAR(13, 17, 139)
190    GOTO 190
```

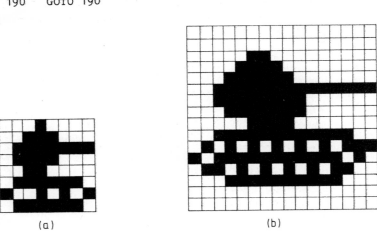

Fig. 2.6. (a) Small tank. (b) Large tank.

It is worth noting that if the codes used for the four parts of the tank all belong to the same set, then any colour assignment that is used always gives the same colour to each part.

In general, large images can be designed as a set of adjacent characters. Making sure that the characters all belong to the same set simplifies the task of assigning colours to the parts of a large image and of displaying it with a unified colour scheme.

Simple animation

The graphics features we have examined are sufficient for us to create a simple animated display. Suppose we want the small tank created in Figure 2.6(a) to move successively to the different positions along a row as shown in Figure 2.7. This movement

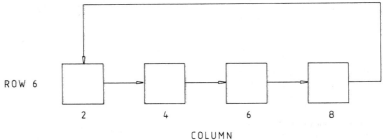

Fig. 2.7. Movement pattern.

sequence can be created by plotting the tank in one of the positions, leaving it there for a short time, blanking it out with a space (which has code 32) and immediately plotting it in the next position. Following this process repeatedly gives the illusion of movement. A program for this is:

```
100     CALL CLEAR
110     CALL CHAR(128, "10387F78307CAA7C")
120     CALL SCREEN(12)
130     CALL COLOR(13, 2, 1)
140     ROW=6
150     COLUMN=2
160     CALL HCHAR(ROW, COLUMN, 128)
170     FOR J=1 TO 100
180     NEXT J
190     CALL HCHAR(ROW, COLUMN, 32)
200     COLUMN=COLUMN+2
210     IF COLUMN=10 THEN 150
220     GOTO 160
```

Lines 170 and 180 provide a delay. Decreasing or increasing the number 200 in line 170 speeds up or slows down the motion correspondingly.

An alternative way of creating this effect is to plot invisible tanks at each position where a tank is to appear and then to make the tank visible for a time and then invisible again at its successive positions. This necessitates defining the tank as four separate characters, otherwise the tanks in each of the four positions cannot be manipulated individually. The following program creates the motion in this way.

```
100     CALL CLEAR
110     CALL SCREEN(12)
120     A$="10387F78307CAA7C"
130     FOR J=128 TO 152 STEP 8
140     CALL CHAR(J, A$)
150     NEXT J
160     FOR K=13 TO 16
170     CALL COLOR(K, 1, 1)
180     NEXT K
190     CALL HCHAR(6, 2, 128)
200     CALL HCHAR(6, 4, 136)
210     CALL HCHAR(6, 6, 144)
220     CALL HCHAR(6, 8, 152)
230     FOR L=13 TO 16
240     CALL COLOR(L, 2, 1)
250     FOR M=1 TO 200
260     NEXT M
270     CALL COLOR(L, 1, 1)
280     NEXT L
290     GOTO 230
```

If we want the tank to move over a part of the screen that already contains a display in such a way that the original display is restored when the tank has passed, then we can modify the first method. The modification involves the use of the CALL GCHAR statement which enables us to examine any position on the screen to see what is plotted there. The form of this statement is

CALL GCHAR (ROW, COLUMN, VARIABLE)

and when it is executed it causes the ASCII code for the character displayed at the position given by ROW and COLUMN to be assigned to VARIABLE. Thus, if there is an 'A' on the screen at column 2 of row 3, the statement

CALL (3, 2, TEMP)

will cause the value 65 (the code for 'A') to be assigned to the variable TEMP.

In this way, we can examine the position to which the tank is about to move and store the code for the character displayed there so that it can be replaced when the tank moves on. A program to plot the column number of the positions the tank is to occupy and then to make the tank follow the same path as before without destroying them is listed below.

```
100    CALL CLEAR
110    CALL SCREEN(12)
120    CALL CHAR(128, "10387F78307CAA7C")
130    CALL COLOR(13, 2, 1)
140    CALL HCHAR(6, 2, 50)
150    CALL HCHAR(6, 4, 52)
160    CALL HCHAR(6, 6, 54)
170    CALL HCHAR(6, 8, 56)
180    ROW=6
190    COLUMN=2
200    CALL GCHAR(ROW, COLUMN, TEMP)
210    CALL HCHAR(ROW, COLUMN, 128)
220    FOR J=1 TO 200
230    NEXT J
240    CALL HCHAR(ROW, COLUMN, TEMP)
250    COLUMN=COLUMN+2
260    IF COLUMN=10 THEN 190
270    GOTO 200
```

Thus, TI BASIC provides us with the facilities we need to create and examine any display. With CHAR we can create any characters that we need and they can be displayed with HCHAR and VCHAR. The screen can be examined using GCHAR.

On a number of machines the role of HCHAR and VCHAR is played by POKE while that of GCHAR is filled by PEEK. However, the features of TI BASIC are much easier to use than are PEEK and POKE because they allow us to refer to the screen directly and do not require us to know about such things as the location of the screen memory and the screen memory map.

Sound

The computer has an in-built sound generator that can be controlled from TI BASIC. Sounds consisting of up to three tones and one noise played simultaneously can be generated. When a tone is generated the user can specify its duration, its frequency (that is, its pitch) and its volume. When generating noise, its duration, type and volume must be given. The types of noise that can be produced include various kinds of periodic noise and of white noise.

A single tone is generated by using the CALL SOUND statement in the form

CALL SOUND (DURATION, FREQUENCY, VOLUME)

In this statement, DURATION gives the length of the tone in milliseconds (thousandths of a second), FREQUENCY gives its frequency in Hertz (or cycles per second), and VOLUME gives its loudness using numbers from 0 to 30 with 0 indicating the loudest level and 30 the quietest. The maximum value for DURATION is 4250, so that a note can last for up to four and a quarter seconds. The frequency can vary from 110 to 44733 which is from the note A in the octave containing low C to well above the range of human hearing. The User's Reference Guide gives the frequencies corresponding to all the notes in a range of four octaves. With reference to this table, the command for playing middle C at full volume for a quarter of a second can be written as:

CALL SOUND (250, 262, 0)

When used to the full, SOUND permits up to four simultaneous sounds to be produced, and then it takes the form:

CALL SOUND (DURATION, F1, V1, F2, V2, F3, V3, F4, V4)

In fact, anything from one to four pairs of values for frequency and volume can be included. Not more than three of the sounds can be tones, though, and not more than one can be a noise.

In this way, a two-tone chord can be produced by:

CALL SOUND (250, 262, 0, 330, 0)

and a three-note chord by:

CALL SOUND (250, 260, 0, 330, 0, 392, 0)

When DURATION has a positive value, the sound produced does not commence until any existing sound comes to an end. The computer can continue its other actions while it generates sounds. However, giving a negative value to DURATION causes the sound produced to be generated at once, interrupting any sound currently being produced. This can be useful in causing sounds to be generated at a precise time or in generating sound effects.

The noise channel is activated by giving FREQUENCY a negative integer value from -1 to -8. Each value causes a different type of noise to be generated. They are given names in the User's Reference Guide, but they need to be heard to be appreciated or distinguished. A single sound can be generated by:

CALL SOUND (2000, -5, 2)

A sound consisting of a single tone accompanied by noise by:

CALL SOUND (1000, 220, -5, 4)

Finally, to give an example showing all four sound channels in use, a 3-note chord accompanied by noise is generated by:

CALL SOUND (2000, 523, 2, 220, 2, 175, 2, -4, 4)

Sound effects can be generated quite easily. For example, an increasingly loud blast is generated by:

```
100    FOR VOL=30 TO 0 STEP -5
110    CALL SOUND(-100, 523, VOL, 262, VOL)
120    NEXT VOL
```

A tuneless trill that increases in pitch is produced by

```
100    FOR FREQ=220 TO 440 STEP 10
110    CALL SOUND(-100, FREQ, 0)
120    NEXT FREQ
```

Summary

The features of TI BASIC for producing colour graphics and sound have been introduced in this chapter. We have met the statements SCREEN, COLOR, CHAR, HCHAR, VCHAR, GCHAR and SOUND. Examples of their use in producing displays and in generating sound were presented and the techniques introduced here will be used in the programs developed in later chapters.

Chapter Three
Screen Displays

The attractiveness of any program is considerably enhanced by taking care in designing the screen displays that it produces. This is self-evident as far as the display of pictures and images is concerned. It is, however, just as important when a screen full of text is to be displayed. When reading the instructions for playing a game or for using a program of any kind there are few things more off-putting than having to read a screen that is filled to capacity with capital letters all displayed in white on a black background. A little care in arranging the layout and in using colours imaginatively can make even reading instructions enjoyable rather than making it a chore which may well be skipped altogether. In this way it can encourage the users of a program to read the instructions for using it rather than tempting them to start to use the program without having any clear idea of how to drive it.

In short, whatever the display, it can always be improved by the thoughtful use of colour and graphics. It is worth remembering that in almost all instances the screen is the interface between the program and its user. It shows the user what his program is doing at any time.

Placing text on the screen

On nearly all computers the PRINT statement is most commonly used for displaying text on the screen. The TI99/4A, however, has a DISPLAY statement which is purely for displaying items on the screen, so that we shall use DISPLAY for this purpose. It is worth remembering, though, that everything that is true of DISPLAY is also true for PRINT.

When the CALL CLEAR statement is executed, it not only causes the screen to be cleared but it also causes the display position (which is analogous to the print head on a typewriter) to be set to the bottom left corner of the screen. Thus, by clearing the screen in this way we can remove any unwanted items from the screen and also be sure where the next item will be displayed.

A DISPLAY statement causes a list of items to be displayed on the screen. The items of the list must be separated in the DISPLAY statement by at least one of the special separator characters. These are the semicolon, the comma and the colon. A semicolon indicates that the item following it should be printed immediately after the previous one. A comma indicates that the item following it should be displayed starting at the next available position in either column 1 or column 15. A colon indicates that the next item should be displayed at the beginning of the next line.

These rules do not make it particularly easy to control the accurate positioning of messages on the screen. Suppose that in a game we should like to display the current score continually at the bottom left of the screen. We can start by clearing the screen and displaying the score with:

```
200 CALL CLEAR
210 SCORE = 0
220 DISPLAY "THE SCORE IS "; SCORE
```

Later on in the program the score will be increased when a space invader is destroyed or whatever, and the score will be increased and then displayed by lines such as:

```
900 SCORE = SCORE +1
910 GOTO 220
```

Unfortunately, while this causes the new score to be displayed at the bottom of the screen, it also causes the screen to scroll upwards. This pushes the previous score up by one line and causes the previous top line to be lost. Every time the score is increased the screen scrolls up, eventually causing the display for the game itself to vanish completely. This is clearly not what we want.

The only alternative seems to be to clear the screen immediately before the new score is displayed. But if we do this, we shall wipe out the display of the game, thereby disrupting the game, and we shall have to re-create the display each time. This is not satisfactory either. The only solution seems to be for us to write a routine ourselves that allows us to position messages as we would like to.

The CALL HCHAR statement allows us to position a character precisely on the screen provided that we know its code. We propose to use this in developing a routine for displaying a given message starting at a particular screen location.

First, let us store the message itself in the string variable M$ and the row and the column of the starting position in the variables ROW and COLUMN. Thus, in our program we might have the assignments:

    M$ = "THE SCORE IS "
    ROW = 1
    COLUMN = 3

Our routine needs to take the characters in the string assigned to M$, find their ASCII codes and pass them to HCHAR so that it can be used to position each individual character in its proper place on the screen. There is quite a lot of work to do here but, fortunately, TI BASIC provides us with the tools for doing it all.

Since we must take the characters in the string one by one, we should first of all like to know how many characters there are in the string. The function LEN is provided for doing this. It gives the *length* of a string. To show how it is used, after the assignment

    A$ = "STRING"

the command

    DISPLAY LEN (A$)

displays the result 6 because there are six characters in the string assigned to A$, that is, the characters S, T, R, I, N and G. With reference to our assignment to M$, the result of

    DISPLAY LEN (M$)

is 13. This is because apart from ten letters the string contains three spaces, and a space is just as much a character as a letter or a number is. (If you don't believe this, consider that the string would have a rather different appearance if the spaces were absent from it.)

Now that we can find the number of characters in a string, we need to be able to get at each one individually. The function that is provided for taking strings apart is SEG$. Its use is illustrated typically by SEG$ (B$, 2, 3) which gives the part of the string assigned to B$ that starts at character 2 and is 3 characters long. Thus, after the assignment

    B$ = "DALLAS,TEXAS"

the command

DISPLAY SEG$ (B$, 8, 5)

gives TEXAS, and

DISPLAY SEG$ (B$, 2, 3)

gives ALL. In this way, the fourth character of the string can be obtained by SEG$ (B$, 4, 1) and, in general, the Kth character by SEG$ (B$, K, 1). The following program causes the characters of a string to be displayed with one on each line:

```
100    B$ = "DALLAS,TEXAS"
110    DISPLAY B$
120    FOR K=1 TO LEN(B$)
130    DISPLAY SEG$(B$, K, 1)
140    NEXT K
```

The remaining thing that we need to do is to find the ASCII code of a character in a program. BASIC provides the function ASC for this purpose. When given a character string it returns the ASCII code of the first character in the string. Thus:

DISPLAY ASC ("A")

gives 65, while after the assignment

B$ = "BASIC"

the command

DISPLAY ASC (B$)

gives 66, the code for B.

We now have all the tools we need to write a program segment for passing the code of each character in a string to HCHAR so that it can display it in the desired position. It is:

```
2000    FOR K=1 TO LEN(M$)
2010    CH = ASC(SEG$(M$, K, 1))
2020    CALL HCHAR(ROW, COLUMN-1+K, CH)
2030    NEXT K
```

This works properly as long as the message can be displayed on one line along the specified row. If it is too long to do this, it must be made to continue on the next row. To do this, we must find when the message reaches the end of a row and then direct it to the next row. This can be done by:

```
2000    FOR K=1 TO LEN(M$)
```

```
2010    CH = ASC(SEG$(M$, K, 1))
2020    IF COLUMN-1+K <= 32 THEN 2050
2030    ROW=ROW + 1
2040    COLUMN = COLUMN - 32
2050    CALL HCHAR(ROW, COLUMN-1+K, CH)
2060    NEXT K
```

We are still not quite at the end of the road, for our original example displayed not only the message "THE SCORE IS" but also the score itself with the statement:

DISPLAY "THE SCORE IS "; SCORE

Our method of display depends on the message to be displayed being given as a *character string*. It cannot deal with numeric values. Our way around this is to use the function STR$ which is specifically intended for converting numbers to strings. The value of STR$ (16) is the string of two characters "16". Similarly, STR$ (1.75) gives the four character string "1.75". With this function we can express the score itself as a string. All we need now is a way to combine "THE SCORE IS " and STR$ (SCORE) into a single string. This can be done using &, which permits two strings to be combined. The value of A$ & B$ is the string assigned to A$ followed by the string assigned to B$. To illustrate, after the assignments

A$ = "SHREVE"
B$ = "PORT"

The command

DISPLAY A$ & B$

gives SHREVEPORT.

Thus, we can get the required display by making the assignment

M$ = "THE SCORE IS " & STR$ (SCORE)

prior to using the display routine.

Although the development of this routine has taken quite a long time, the routine itself is quite short because of the way that it uses the BASIC functions. In fact, as a final step, it is useful to write it as a *subroutine* because in this way we have provided a utility that can be called by any program that needs it. A subroutine is a sub-program that can be called from a main program. When a main program requires the same task to be performed several times at various points in the program, it is easier to write a subroutine for the task and call it when it is needed than to write out the statements for the task every time it is needed in the main program. Subroutines can also be used to impart structure to a large program by splitting it into smaller parts. This is discussed more fully in Chapter 4.

A subroutine is called from a main program by a statement of the form

GOSUB number

where 'number' gives the line number of the first line in the subroutine. Placing a RETURN statement in the subroutine ensures that control passes back from the subroutine to the main program. The return is to the statement following the one that called the subroutine.

The display subroutine is:

```
2000    FOR K=1 TO LEN(M$)
2010    CH = ASC(SEG$(M$, K, 1))
2020    IF COLUMN-1+K <= 32 THEN 2050
2030    ROW=ROW + 1
2040    COLUMN = COLUMN - 32
2050    CALL HCHAR(ROW, COLUMN-1+K, CH)
2060    NEXT K
2160    RETURN
```

It expects to find the necessary values in M\$, ROW and COLUMN when it is called, and it is called by

GOSUB 2000

Placing other characters on the screen

Since our display subroutine handles characters and is in no way specific to dealing with text it can be used to position any kind of character on the screen. Graphics characters can be handled in just the same way as letters. The only prerequisite to using the display subroutine for plotting characters is to present them to it having been assigned to the string variable M\$.

All the characters appearing on the keyboard can be typed directly into an assignment statement, so that there is no problem in making an assignment such as:

M\$ = "1 2 3 & \$ % 7 8 9"

to display these characters. This only leaves us with the problem of dealing with *user-defined characters*.

Suppose that three characters have been defined in a program and have been assigned the codes 128, 129 and 130. To display these three characters alongside each other we need to be able to assign them to the variable M$. This can be done using the CHR$ function because, as a typical example, CHR$ (128) gives the character with code 128. In this way, the character can be displayed directly by

DISPLAY CHR$ (128)

or assigned to a string variable with

A$ = CHR$ (128)

Our problem is solved by the assignment

M$ = CHR$ (128) & CHR$ (129) & CHR$ (130)

It should be mentioned that any characters, and not just the user-defined ones, can be dealt with in this way. It is also worth mentioning that the functions CHR$ and ASC are the opposites of each other in that when CHR$ is given a code it returns the character with that code whereas when ASC is given a character it returns the code for that character. Another way of seeing this is to observe that:

DISPLAY CHR$ (ASC ("+"))

gives + because it displays the character whose code is the code for +. Similarly,

DISPLAY ASC (CHR$ (65))

gives 65 because it displays the code of the character whose code is 65.

Designing a display

This section provides an illustration of how the ideas we have developed so far can be used to produce a simple display with which the user can interact. The illustration shows how the screen can be used as a form to be filled in interactively. The instructions for filling in the form are given at the top of the screen. Any wrongly typed entries can be corrected simply by entering them again. When the form is filled to the user's satisfaction this can be indicated to the computer. The ways in which the information once entered could be stored in a file so that it is saved permanently are covered in Chapter 7.

The appearance of the display is shown in Figure 3.1. The program must first create this display with the instructions at the top and the labels in each box. Then it must scan the keyboard to see if a

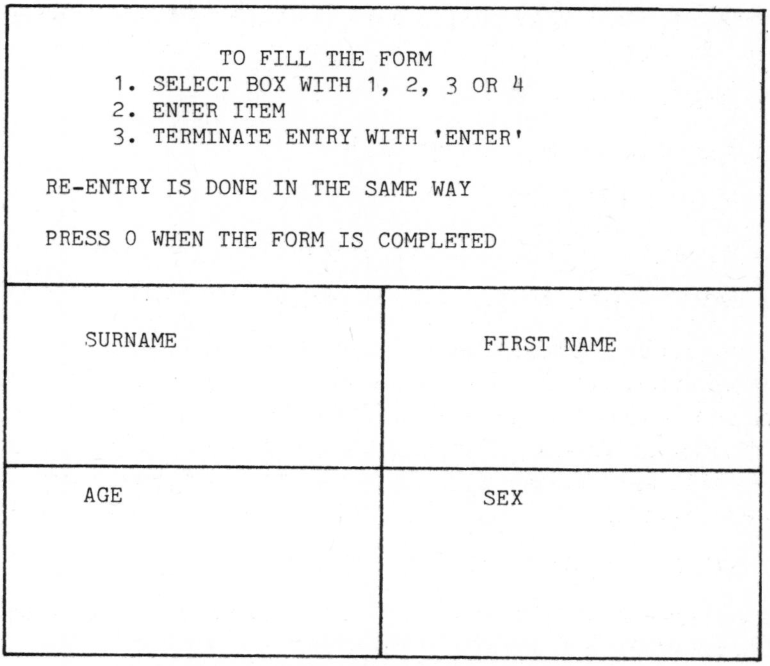

```
                    TO FILL THE FORM
          1. SELECT BOX WITH 1, 2, 3 OR 4
          2. ENTER ITEM
          3. TERMINATE ENTRY WITH 'ENTER'

RE-ENTRY IS DONE IN THE SAME WAY

PRESS 0 WHEN THE FORM IS COMPLETED
```

SURNAME	FIRST NAME
AGE	SEX

Fig. 3.1. Appearance of the form on the screen.

key has been pressed. If a key from 1 to 4 has been pressed, then any existing entry in the appropriate box must be wiped out (in case we are correcting an error), and a cursor appears to give a visual response to indicate where the next input is to be placed. The input is then accepted and placed in its box. If the zero key is pressed the program terminates. All other keys are ignored.

The initial display can be created by:

```
CALL CLEAR
CALL SCREEN (8)
CALL COLOR (13, 2, 1)
CALL CHAR (128, "FF")
CALL CHAR (129, "0101010101010101")
CALL CHAR (130, "FF010101010101010101")
CALL HCHAR (10, 1, 128, 32)
CALL HCHAR (18, 1, 128, 32)
```

```
CALL VCHAR (10, 16, 129, 14)
CALL HCHAR (10, 16, 130)
CALL HCHAR (18, 16, 130)
```

The instructions and labels can be added, using the display subroutine, by:

```
M$="TO FILL THE FORM"
ROW = 1
COLUMN = 8
GOSUB 2000
M$ = "1.SELECT BOX WITH 1, 2, 3 OR 4"
ROW = 3
COLUMN = 2
GOSUB 2000
M$ = "2.ENTER ITEM"
ROW = 4
COLUMN = 2
GOSUB 2000
    .
    .
    .
```

and so on. Although the placing of the labels must be planned initially at this level of detail, the programming is clearly repetitive. It can be presented more compactly as:

```
FOR J = 1 TO 10
READ M$, ROW, COLUMN
GOSUB 2000
NEXT J
DATA "TO FILL THE FORM", 1, 8
DATA "1.SELECT BOX WITH 1, 2, 3 OR 4", 3, 2
DATA "2.ENTER ITEM", 4, 2
    .
    .
    .
```

and so on to include all the remaining DATA statements.

Next, the keyboard must be scanned, and the appropriate action taken for the keys 0 to 4 while all other keys are ignored. This can be done by

```
500    CALL KEY(0, CODE, STATUS)
510    IF STATUS = 0 THEN 500
```

```
520    IF CODE=ASC("0") THEN 1590
530    IF CODE=ASC("1") THEN 1000
540    IF CODE=ASC("2") THEN 1100
550    IF CODE=ASC("3") THEN 1200
560    IF CODE=ASC("4") THEN 1300
570    GOTO 500
1000   ROW=14
1010   COLUMN=3
1020   GOTO 1500
1100   ROW=14
1110   COLUMN=18
1120   GOTO 1500
1200   ROW=22
1210   COLUMN=3
1220   GOTO 1500
1300   ROW=22
1310   COLUMN=18
1320   GOTO 1500
1500   CALL HCHAR(ROW, COLUMN, 32,10)
1510   CALL HCHAR(ROW, COLUMN, 30)
1520   CALL HCHAR(ROW, COLUMN, 32)
1530   CALL KEY(0, CODE, STATUS)
1540   IF STATUS=0 THEN 1510
1550   IF CODE=13 THEN 500
1560   CALL HCHAR(ROW, COLUMN, CODE)
1570   COLUMN=COLUMN + 1
1580   GOTO 1530
1590   END
```

In the final section of this program from line 1500 to 1590, line 1500 blanks out the previous entry in any box by plotting ten spaces, so that for the purposes of this program we are assuming that no entry is longer than ten characters. Line 1510 plots the cursor, which has the code 30, and line 1520 blanks it out, making it flash. The code for ENTER is 13, and line 1550 detects when ENTER is pressed to terminate an entry. Lines 1560 and 1570 place the entries on the screen character by character in a simple fashion which we can use since we have assumed that no entry is long enough to reach the end of its row.

The section from line 500 to the end of the program can be simplified, as well it might be. It contains rather a lot of GOTO statements that make it none too easy to follow. The main simplification can be achieved by attending to the IF ... THEN statements. In our program, we should like to be able to include conditional statements with the form:

IF (CODE < 48) OR (CODE > 52) THEN

This is not possible in TI BASIC. However, by resorting to

something of a trick we can construct an equivalent feature.

When TI BASIC deals with a conditional statement of the general form:

IF condition THEN line number

the condition part can be a logical expression involving a relation or a numeric expression. When it is a numeric expression, the expression is evaluated and a zero result is treated in the same way as false while any non-zero result is treated as true. Similarly, when dealing with a logical expression, zero is used to represent its being false and any non-zero value represents its being true. Now the truth table for the OR operator is:

A	B	A OR B
FALSE	FALSE	FALSE
FALSE	TRUE	TRUE
TRUE	FALSE	TRUE
TRUE	TRUE	TRUE

The addition table for zero and non-zero values is:

X	Y	X + Y
zero	zero	zero
zero	non-zero	non-zero
non-zero	zero	non-zero
non-zero	non-zero	non-zero

If we observe that both tables have the same pattern, we can conclude that as a consequence of the way in which truth values are represented we can use addition to represent the OR operator. This means that where we would like to write:

IF (CODE < 48) OR (CODE > 52) THEN

we can achieve the same effect by writing

IF (CODE <48) + (CODE > 52) THEN

The AND operator can be dealt with in a similar way. The truth table for AND is:

A	B	A AND B
FALSE	FALSE	FALSE
FALSE	TRUE	FALSE
TRUE	FALSE	FALSE
TRUE	TRUE	TRUE

The multiplication table for zero and non-zero values follows exactly the same pattern. It is:

X	Y	X * Y
zero	zero	zero
zero	non-zero	zero
non-zero	zero	zero
non-zero	non-zero	non-zero

The consequence of this correspondence is that we can use multiplication to represent the AND operator. Thus, where we might like to write:

IF (CODE >128) AND (COLOUR$ = "BLUE") THEN

we can write

IF (CODE > 128)*(COLOUR$ = "BLUE") THEN

See Appendix 3 for a fuller explanation of logic and logical expressions.

Using conditional statements with the simulated OR operator, the section of the program for scanning the keyboard and responding appropriately can be rewritten more compactly as follows:

```
500    CALL KEY(0, CODE, STATUS)
510    IF (STATUS = 0)+(CODE < 48)+(CODE > 52) THEN 500
520    IF CODE=ASC("0") THEN 680
530    ROW=14
540    IF (CODE=49)+(CODE=50) THEN 560
550    ROW=22
560    COLUMN=3
```

```
570   IF (CODE=49)+(CODE=51) THEN 590
580   COLUMN=18
590   CALL HCHAR(ROW, COLUMN, 32,10)
600   CALL HCHAR(ROW, COLUMN, 30)
610   CALL HCHAR(ROW, COLUMN, 32)
620   CALL KEY(0, CODE, STATUS)
630   IF STATUS=0 THEN 600
640   IF CODE=13 THEN 500
650   CALL HCHAR(ROW, COLUMN, CODE)
660   COLUMN=COLUMN + 1
670   GOTO 600
680   END
```

Screen patterns

We have already seen that it is a simple matter to fill the screen with a single character, and the use of a single specially designed character can by itself produce an attractive display. Figure 3.2 gives an

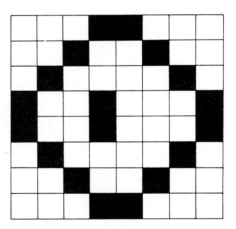

Fig. 3.2. An octagonal character.

example of a character that is well suited for this purpose. A program to fill the screen with it is:

```
100   CALL CLEAR
110   CALL SCREEN(8)
120   CALL COLOR(13, 2, 1)
130   CALL CHAR(128, "1824429191422418")
140   CALL HCHAR(1, 1, 128, 24*32)
150   GOTO 150
```

However, more varied displays than this can be created by using some rule to compute the code for the character to be placed at each position on the screen. We can, for example, produce the equivalent of a contour map as found in an atlas if we have a rule giving the height at each screen position, such as:

HEIGHT = ROW + COLUMN

Then, by representing different ranges of values of HEIGHT by differently coloured characters, we can plot a contour map on the screen. Using the rule just given, we can note that since ROW varies from 1 to 24 and COLUMN from 1 to 32, the values of HEIGHT range from 2 to 56. Thus, we can divide the range of values of HEIGHT into four intervals, each to be represented by a different colour as shown in the following Table 3.1.

Table 3.1. The colours used for the intervals of HEIGHT.

Range of values	Colour
2 – 14	Light green
15 – 28	Dark green
29 – 42	Light yellow
43 – 56	Medium red

A program to produce the map is:

```
100    CALL CLEAR
110    A$="FFFFFFFFFFFFFFFF"
120    CALL COLOR(13, 4, 1)
130    CALL COLOR(14, 13, 1)
140    CALL COLOR(15, 12, 1)
150    CALL COLOR(16, 9, 1)
160    FOR J=128 TO 152 STEP 8
170    CALL CHAR(J, A$)
180    NEXT J
190    FOR ROW=1 TO 24
200    FOR COLUMN=1 TO 32
210    HEIGHT=ROW + COLUMN
220    IF HEIGHT <= 14 THEN 270
230    IF HEIGHT <= 28 THEN 290
240    IF HEIGHT <= 42 THEN 310
250    CODE=152
260    GOTO 320
270    CODE=128
280    GOTO 320
```

```
290    CODE=136
300    GOTO 320
310    CODE=144
320    CALL HCHAR(ROW, COLUMN, CODE)
330    NEXT COLUMN
340    NEXT ROW
350    GOTO 350
```

If the transitions between the colours in this display strike you as too sharp, then they can be blurred somewhat by using suitably designed characters. For example, a better character to represent the range from 29 to 42 might be one with alternate dark green and medium red dots defined by:

CALL CHAR (144, "55AA55AA55AA55AA")
CALL COLOR (15, 13, 9)

There is tremendous scope here for experimenting with different divisions of the range of HEIGHT and for designing characters to give the display with the greatest effect.

We can amend the last program quite easily to create a display that is circular in character rather than diagonal. This time HEIGHT is given by changing line 210 to:

```
210    HEIGHT=(ROW - 12)^2 + (COLUMN - 16)^2
```

Its values range from 0 to 400. If we use the same colours as before, but this time to represent the divisions 0 – 50, 51 – 100, 101 –200 and 201 – 400 then lines 220 to 240 must be changed to:

```
220    IF HEIGHT <= 50 THEN 270
230    IF HEIGHT <= 100 THEN 290
240    IF HEIGHT <= 200 THEN 310
```

The resulting new program should help to make it clear that our program provides a framework for creating any number of screen patterns by systematically assigning a specially designed character to each position on the screen.

Summary

In this chapter we have developed methods for creating interesting displays composed of text, graphics or a mixture of both. At the same time we have introduced a number of the features of TI BASIC and indicated how they can be used. These features include

DISPLAY, LEN, SEG$, ASC, STR$, CHR$ and GOSUB. We have also developed some utility routines to make up for shortcomings in TI BASIC.

Chapter Four
Program Development

In this book, we are trying to adopt a systematic approach to program development at all times. The purpose of this is to make the programs presented in subsequent chapters as easy to understand as possible, and also to make them as easy as possible to amend or extend in any way that the reader may care to. The approach to program development that we shall adopt is known as *top-down design*. Extensive use is made of subroutines to break a program down into smaller parts. Remarks are used liberally, particularly to identify the purposes of subroutines, but also to identify the components in any rather long sequence of BASIC statements.

Top-down design

When designing a program in top-down fashion, the program is specified first at the top level as a set of tasks which must be accomplished in some order so that the program may achieve its stated purpose. In this way the structure of the program can be made quite clear. In general, a task will be accomplished by calling a subroutine to perform it. However, it may be that some of the tasks are quite complex and can be broken down further into sub-tasks. In this case a subroutine called at the top level in the program will itself call further subroutines. The process of task refinement may go on to some depth. It will be reflected in the program by subroutines that call subroutines, and so on. When it actually comes to writing the BASIC statements for a particular sub-task this should be quite an easy matter, since any end sub-task should be small and therefore easy to program.

The idea can probably be made clearer with an example than by a general discussion, so let us consider how we might go about writing a program for a particular application. Suppose that we want to read text from some input device, divide it into words and then do particular things with any words that begin with X, Y or Z. At the top level, the division into tasks can be accomplished in this way:

Initialise
Repeatedly
   Get a word
   Take special actions for words starting with X, Y or Z
Until all words are read

The application now consists of two tasks to be carried out repeatedly. They are preceded by an initialisation stage, but this cannot be written until we have decided on the details of how the two tasks are to be accomplished. Therefore, neglecting the initialisation stage for the moment, a program for the application which reflects the structure we have chosen could be

```
200     GOSUB 1000
210     GOSUB 2000
220     GOTO 200
230     END
```

where the subroutine starting at line 1000 is for getting a word and the one starting at line 2000 is for taking the special actions.

If we decide that the task of getting a word is a single task that is not worth splitting into sub-tasks, then there is no further refinement needed for this task. The task for taking the special actions can probably be usefully divided into sub-tasks, though. Suppose that the actions to be taken when a word starting with one of the special letters is found are to count all the words starting with X, to store all the words beginning with Y, and to display any words beginning with Z. The task then has the form:

Find first letter of the word
If it is X then count it
If it is Y then store it
If it is Z then display it

By making the counting, storing and displaying into sub-tasks, we can write the subroutine for this task as:

```
2000    FIRST$=SEG$(WORD$, 1, 1)
2010    IF FIRST$="X" THEN 2100
2020    IF FIRST$="Y" THEN 2200
2030    IF FIRST$="Z" THEN 2300
2040    RETURN
```

where starting at line 2100 we have the routine for counting, at 2200 that for storing, and at 2300 that for displaying. We would like these routines to be written as subroutines, but in this case it is easier to write them as sections of code within the same subroutine. The reason for this is the rather restricted form of the IF statement in TI BASIC.

Notice that in writing this subroutine, we are assuming that the first subroutine leaves any word that it has found in the variable WORD$, so that we have established how the two subroutines communicate with each other. We can write a very simple version of the first subroutine for finding words so that we end up with a complete working program. We shall cheat a little by making it read words from a data list so that it is not really as powerful as our original specification suggested that it should be. The simple version of the subroutine is:

```
1000    READ WORD$
1010    IF WORD$="END" THEN 230
1020    DATA AYE, ZERO, BEE, XYLOPHONE, SEA, YOU
1030    DATA DEED, ARE, ZEST, END
1040    RETURN
```

At this stage, we have written the main program and the subroutines for its tasks, but we have not written the routines for the end sub-tasks. A consequence of not having written the end sub-tasks is that we cannot yet write the initialisation stage either. Without writing the routines for the sub-tasks, it is possible to test the program as it is developed so far to ensure that its structure is properly designed. By including dummy versions of the unwritten routines we can ensure that they are called in the way that they should be. For example, rather than writing the routine to count all the words starting with X, we can include the dummy statement:

2100 DISPLAY "COUNT"

By putting together all the program segments that we have written so far, and including the dummy routines, we can get the following:

```
200     GOSUB 1000
210     GOSUB 2000
220     GOTO 200
230     END
1000    READ WORD$
1010    IF WORD$="END" THEN 230
1020    DATA AYE, ZERO, BEE, XYLOPHONE, SEA, YOU
1030    DATA DEED, ARE, ZEST, END
```

```
1040    RETURN
2000    FIRST$=SEG$(WORD$, 1, 1)
2010    IF FIRST$="X" THEN 2100
2020    IF FIRST$="Y" THEN 2200
2030    IF FIRST$="Z" THEN 2300
2040    RETURN
2100    DISPLAY "COUNT"
2110    RETURN
2200    DISPLAY "STORE"
2210    RETURN
2300    DISPLAY "DISPLAY"
2310    RETURN
```

Having run this program and gained the confidence that we have a program the structure of which is correct, we can proceed to complete it by writing the BASIC statements for performing the end sub-tasks. If we decide that the variable XCOUNT is to be used to hold the count of the number of words starting with X, that the words starting with Y are to be stored in an array named Y$, and that words starting with Z are to be displayed using the DISPLAY statement, then we can write not only the routines but also the initialisation stage. The routines are, for the counting:

2100 XCOUNT = XCOUNT + 1

for the storing:

2200 Y$(I) = WORD$
2210 I = I + 1

and for the displaying:

2300 DISPLAY WORD$

At this stage the complete program can be listed. However, if we simply list it in exactly the same way as the version that we used to test that the structure of the program was satisfactory, it will be just as unreadable as that was. The program can be made easier to read and easier to understand by adding remarks to it. A line that starts with REM can contain any remark that we care to make. Remarks are completely ignored by the computer when the program containing them is run.

We shall use *remarks* to indicate the purposes of the sections of a program and of subroutines. A remark (REM) will always be placed before the part of the program to which it relates. With a subroutine, we shall introduce a line or lines immediately before the start of the subroutine to state its purpose. Thus, typically, for the subroutine starting at line 1000, the explanation is given on line 999. It is considered poor style to jump to a remark as the first line of a subroutine. One reason for this is that utility programs do exist to remove the remarks from other programs, thereby reducing the amount of storage needed when they are run. We shall also use remarks to provide a gap between a program and its subroutines, and between the subroutines themselves.

When listing a program we shall always adopt the arrangement that the main program is listed first, followed by its first-level subroutines, then by the second-level subroutines, and so on. When our program is presented in this way and remarks are added to it, the listing becomes:

```
100    REM DEALING WITH WORDS
110    REM *** INITIALISATION ***
120    DIM Y$(100)
130    I=1
140    XCOUNT=0
190    REM *** MAIN PROGRAM LOOP ***
200    GOSUB 1000
210    GOSUB 2000
220    GOTO 200
230    END
998    REM
999    REM SUBROUTINE TO GET A WORD
1000   READ WORD$
1010   IF WORD$="END" THEN 230
1020   DATA AYE, ZERO, BEE, XYLOPHONE, SEA, YOU
1030   DATA DEED, ARE, ZEST, END
1040   RETURN
1998   REM
1999   REM SUBROUTINE FOR SPECIAL WORDS
2000   FIRST$=SEG$(WORD$, 1, 1)
2010   IF FIRST$="X" THEN 2100
2020   IF FIRST$="Y" THEN 2200
2030   IF FIRST$="Z" THEN 2300
2040   RETURN
2099   REM COUNT
2100   XCOUNT=XCOUNT+1
2110   RETURN
2199   REM STORE
2200   Y$(I)=WORD$
2210   I=I+1
2220   RETURN
2299   REM DISPLAY
2300   DISPLAY WORD$
2310   RETURN
```

This listing illustrates the style in which we shall present programs in subsequent chapters. Of course, the reader may or may not choose to adopt this style, but the inclusion of remarks in a consistent way does help to make programs easier to understand, although the use of remarks can be overdone.

Debugging aids

Just in case a systematic approach to program development should fail to produce a properly working program, TI BASIC provides two debugging aids to help in finding what is wrong with the program.

The first is provided by the command

TRACE

which causes a program to display the output that it would give normally but also to display the line number of each statement in the program as it is executed. In this way, a trace shows the order in which the statements of a program are being executed. This permits a check to be made on matters such as whether a program calls its subroutines correctly or if the program is stuck in a loop. Once invoked, tracing remains in force until it is terminated with the command

UNTRACE

The second aid is BREAK, and this permits a program to be stopped at a specified line so that the state of the computation can be examined, for example by looking at the values of variables. A breakpoint can be set with a command such as

BREAK 200

which causes the program to halt immediately before line 200 is executed. Multiple breakpoints can be set with a command such as

BREAK 200, 300, 450

The execution of a program can be resumed after it has been stopped at a breakpoint by issuing the command

CONTINUE

Once invoked, breakpoints remain in force until they are cancelled with the command

UNBREAK

Breakpoints can also be set with a program statement such as:

    10 BREAK 200

Summary

The top-down method of developing programs and the style in which the programs will be presented in later chapters have both been presented and explained. By developing a program in a systematic way and by adding remarks to it in a consistent fashion the programs will be as easy to understand and to amend as is possible. The debugging aids BREAK and TRACE that are provided by TI BASIC have also been described.

Chapter Five
Tiles, Tiling And A Puzzle

Tiling a floor or a wall with square tiles is something that most of us have either done or seen the results. Many intriguing patterns can be created by using comparatively simple decorated tiles. We are in a position to create the same sort of patterns with the computer. We can design graphics characters using CALL CHAR in a way similar to that in which a pattern for a tile is designed. We can also place a character on the screen in a way that is entirely comparable, in terms of the visual result, to when a tile is placed on a wall. In fact, graphics characters are sometimes referred to as *tiles*. We have seen an example of tiling already in one of the 'screen patterns' of Chapter 3. We are aiming here to develop some more designs for tiles which, when displayed, will produce interesting and perhaps unexpected patterns. The example in Chapter 3 has already produced one unexpected pattern in that covering the screen with an essentially octagonal tile also caused diamonds to appear.

Regular tiling

Thinking in terms of tiles, suppose that we want to tile an area using tiles entirely of one shape. There are only three shapes with which this can be done, and they are the square, triangular and hexagonal shapes shown in Figure 5.1.

Now, the problem in designing graphics characters for producing displays with these appearances is that we are restricted to working with characters based on a square. To design a shape to produce the square pattern of Figure 5.1(a) is clearly the easiest task. This pattern will be produced when the screen is filled with the character having shape description "FF818181818181FF" shown in Figure 5.2(a), although it may be less clear that the 'inverted L' of Figure 5.2(b) which has shape description "FF80808080808080" will do just

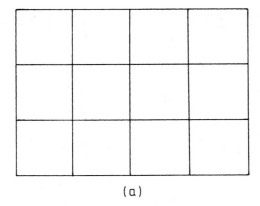

(a)

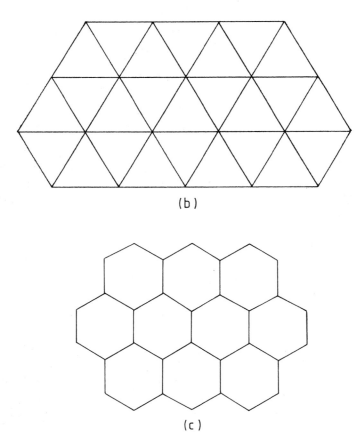

(b)

(c)

Fig. 5.1. Regular coverings. (a) Square. (b) Triangular. (c) Hexagonal.

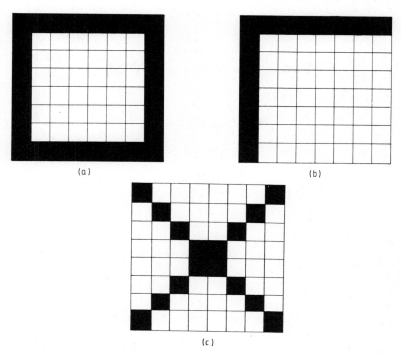

Fig. 5.2. (a) Square character. (b) Inverted L-shaped character. (c) X-shaped character.

as well. The program scheme for placing one of these shapes at every screen position to produce the overall pattern is essentially that given in Chapter 3. We repeat it here as we shall use it as the basis of several variations. It is

```
100    CALL CLEAR
110    CALL SCREEN(8)
120    CALL COLOR(13, 2, 1)
130    CALL CHAR(128, "FF80808080808080")
140    CALL HCHAR(1, 1, 128, 24*32)
150    GOTO 150
```

An equivalent effect can be obtained by filling the screen with the X-shaped character of Figure 5.2(c) which has the shape description "8142241818244281". This fills the screen with diamonds, but a diamond is a square turned through 45 degrees, so although it is rotated we have produced the square pattern again, but in a slightly unexpected way.

The triangular and hexagonal patterns are a little more difficult to generate. However, if we define a character with the shape shown in

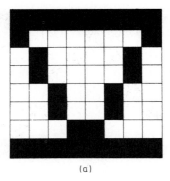 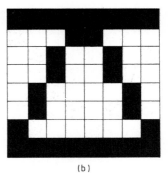

(a)   (b)

Fig. 5.3. (a) Basic character for triangular covering. (b) Inverse of (a).

Figure 5.3(a) having the description "FF814242242418FF" and another having the shape obtained by turning this upside down as in Figure 5.3(b), which has shape description "FF182424424281FF", then we can produce the triangular mesh by filling alternate lines with each character. (Having two characters available, one of which is the other upside down is only equivalent to providing the capability that someone laying tiles has of laying a tile directly or rotating it by 180 degrees before laying it.)

The program for producing this pattern plots the original character in the odd-numbered rows and the inverted one in the even-numbered rows. The program is:

```
100    CALL CLEAR
110    CALL SCREEN(8)
120    CALL COLOR(13, 2, 1)
130    CALL CHAR(128, "FF814242242418FF")
140    CALL CHAR(129, "FF182424424281FF")
150    FOR ROW=1 TO 23 STEP 2
160    CALL HCHAR(ROW, 1, 128, 32)
170    CALL HCHAR(ROW+1, 1, 129, 32)
180    NEXT ROW
190    GOTO 190
```

The hexagonal pattern can be produced (unexpectedly?) by the same program with the Y-shaped character shown in Figure 5.4(a) having shape description "8080412222140808" and its inverse as shown in Figure 5.4(b).

Other patterns

Geometry can provide us with many other patterns of a similar

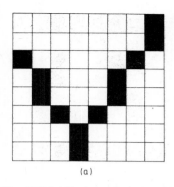 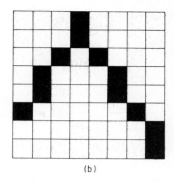

Fig. 5.4. (a) Y-shaped character for hexagonal covering. (b) Inverse of (a).

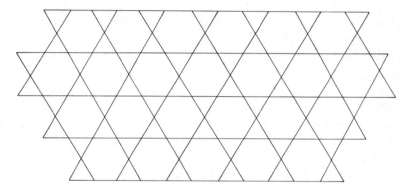

Fig. 5.5. A pattern.

nature to those we have created already. These patterns are often to be seen on wallpaper and floor coverings. One that is commonly used in this way is shown in Figure 5.5. It can be obtained by repeatedly alternating lines filled with the two characters shown in Figure 5.6 which have shape descriptions "FF424281814242FF"

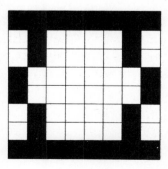 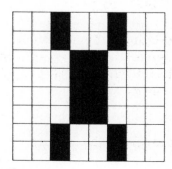

Fig. 5.6. Characters for a repetitive pattern.

and "2424181818182424". At this stage, the resolution of the screen is starting to become a problem, but if you examine this display carefully you can see hexagons, triangles and even Stars of David.

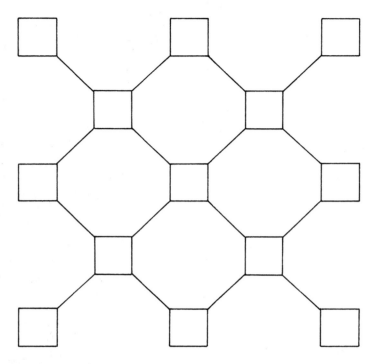

Fig. 5.7. A pattern.

The pattern of Figure 5.7 can be obtained by plotting alternately the character with shape description "81423C24243C4281" shown in Figure 5.8 and a space. A program for this is:

```
100    CALL CLEAR
110    CALL SCREEN(8)
120    CALL COLOR(13, 2, 1)
130    CALL CHAR(130, "81423C24243C4281")
140    FOR ROW=1 TO 24
150    FOR COLUMN=1 TO 32
160    SUM=ROW + COLUMN
170    IF (2*INT(SUM/2))=SUM THEN 180 ELSE 190
180    CALL HCHAR(ROW, COLUMN, 130)
190    NEXT COLUMN
200    NEXT ROW
210    GOTO 210
```

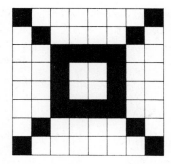

Fig. 5.8. Character for an unexpected pattern.

Plotting the character with shape description "0C0C3F3FFCFC3030" shown in Figure 5.9(b) at every screen position gives a remarkable effect because the backgrounds combine to produce the foreground shape in reverse, that is, facing in the opposite direction. The effect is even more unexpected when rotated through 45 degrees. Filling the screen with character shown in Figure 5.9(a) which has shape description "007C445C507C14F7" produces a 'swastika frieze'. These last two examples are based on patterns from Islamic art, which can supply just as many interesting and pleasing patterns as can geometry.

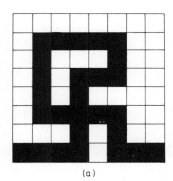

(a)

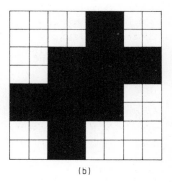

(b)

Fig. 5.9. (a) Character for a swastika frieze. (b) Character for a pattern with an inverse background.

Moving patterns

In this section we shall create a pattern, and then develop methods for making it move as a prelude to developing a puzzle program in the next section. We can create a tile of the shape shown in Figure 5.10 as the building block for our pattern. By associating it with two different codes we shall be able to plot it in two colours. We shall

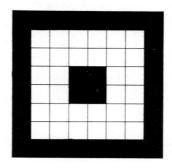

Fig. 5.10. Character for a moving pattern.

then use two arrays to hold the rows and columns occupied by each tile in the pattern. If the pattern is to be a square with five character positions along each side having its top left corner in row 6 and column 10 we can store the position for each character in the pattern by:

```
100    DIM ROW(16),COLUMN(16)
110    FOR K=1 TO 5
120    ROW(K)=6
130    COLUMN(K)=9+K
140    ROW(8+K)=10
150    COLUMN(8+K)=15-K
160    NEXT K
170    FOR J=1 TO 3
180    ROW(5+J)=6+J
190    COLUMN(5+J)=14
200    ROW(13+J)=10-J
210    COLUMN(13+J)=10
220    NEXT J
```

The characters can be defined and given colours by

```
230    CALL CHAR(128, "FF818199998181FF")
240    CALL CHAR(136, "FF818199998181FF")
250    CALL COLOR(13,5,1)
260    CALL COLOR(14,7,1)
```

The square pattern can then be filled with tiles of alternating colours by:

```
270    CALL CLEAR
280    FOR K=1 TO 16
```

```
290    SUM=ROW(K)+COLUMN(K)
300    IF (2*INT(SUM/2))=SUM THEN 310 ELSE 330
310    CALL HCHAR(ROW(K),COLUMN(K),128)
320    GOTO 340
330    CALL HCHAR(ROW(K),COLUMN(K),136)
340    NEXT K
```

We can then make the square move by moving each character to the position occupied by its successor, and doing this repeatedly. It can be done by:

```
350    CALL GCHAR(ROW(1),COLUMN(1),CODE)
360    L=2
370    CALL GCHAR(ROW(L),COLUMN(L),NEXTCODE)
380    CALL HCHAR(ROW(L),COLUMN(L),CODE)
390    CODE=NEXTCODE
400    L=L+1
410    FOR M=1 TO 100
420    NEXT M
430    IF L < 17 THEN 370
440    CALL HCHAR(ROW(1),COLUMN(1),CODE)
450    GOTO 350
```

This completes the program. The delay in lines 410 and 420 can be altered to speed up or slow down the movement.

A puzzle

The puzzle consists of two intersecting square patterns of the kind plotted in the previous section. We shall refer to one square as P and the other as Q. Initially, the square P is made up of 8 blue tiles and 8 green tiles, and square Q is made up entirely of 14 red tiles except for where it intersects with square P. The initial configuration is illustrated in Figure 5.11. The user can rotate at any time one of the squares in a clockwise direction. The idea of the puzzle is to rotate the squares until a position is arrived at in which the tiles in square P are alternately blue and red, while those of square Q are alternately green and red.

Thus, the form of the program for this puzzle is:

Plot the squares
Repeatedly
    Accept a request to move a square
    Move a square accordingly

The program listing for the puzzle is given as Figure 5.12. The square

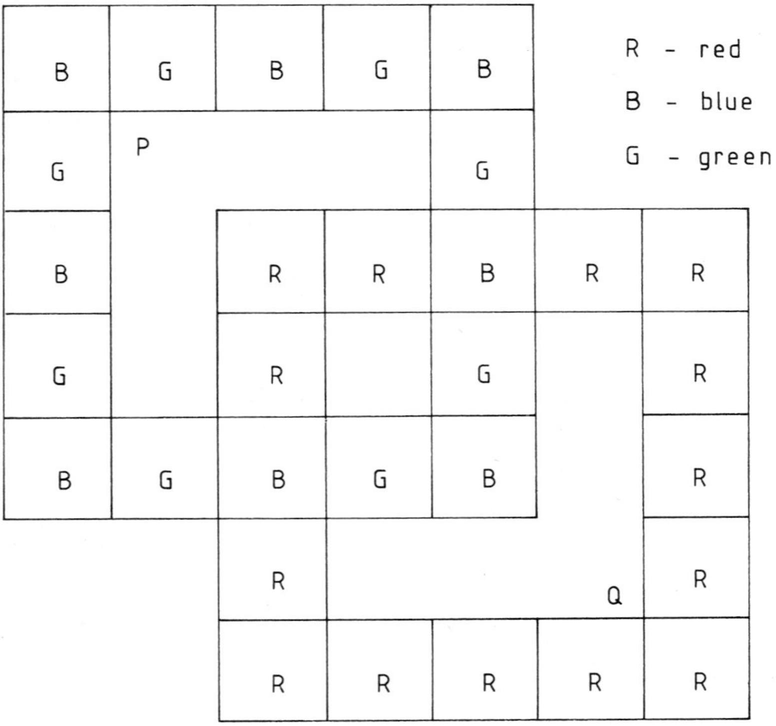

B	G	B	G	B		

Fig. 5.11. Initial configuration for puzzle.

labelled P can be rotated by pressing P and the square Q can be caused to rotate by pressing Q.

```
100    REM PUZZLE
110    REM *** PLOT SQUARES ***
120    DIM PROW(16),PCOLUMN(16),QROW(16),QCOLUMN(16)
130    FOR K=1 TO 5
140    PROW(K)=6
150    PCOLUMN(K)=9+K
160    PROW(8+K)=10
170    PCOLUMN(8+K)=15-K
180    NEXT K
190    FOR J=1 TO 3
200    PROW(5+J)=6+J
210    PCOLUMN(5+J)=14
220    PROW(13+J)=10-J
230    PCOLUMN(13+J)=10
240    NEXT J
250    FOR K=1 TO 16
260    QROW(K)=PROW(K)+2
270    QCOLUMN(K)=PCOLUMN(K)+2
```

```
280    NEXT K
290    A$="FF818199998181FF"
300    CALL CHAR(128, A$)
310    CALL CHAR(136, A$)
320    CALL CHAR(144, A$)
330    CALL COLOR(13,5,1)
340    CALL COLOR(14,7,1)
350    CALL COLOR(15,13,1)
360    CALL CLEAR
370    FOR K=1 TO 16
380    CALL HCHAR(QROW(K),QCOLUMN(K),136)
390    NEXT K
400    FOR K=1 TO 16
410    SUM=PROW(K)+PCOLUMN(K)
420    IF (2*INT(SUM/2))=SUM THEN 430 ELSE 450
430    CALL HCHAR(PROW(K),PCOLUMN(K),128)
440    GOTO 460
450    CALL HCHAR(PROW(K),PCOLUMN(K),144)
460    NEXT K
470    CALL HCHAR(7,11,ASC("P"))
480    CALL HCHAR(11,15,ASC("Q"))
490    REM REQUEST FOR MOVEMENT
500    CALL KEY(0, CODE, STATUS)
510    IF STATUS=0 THEN 500
520    IF CODE=ASC("P") THEN 600
530    IF CODE=ASC("Q") THEN 800
540    GOTO 500
590    REM ROTATE SQUARE P
600    CALL GCHAR(PROW(1),PCOLUMN(1),CODE)
610    FOR L=2 TO 16
620    CALL GCHAR(PROW(L),PCOLUMN(L),NEXTCODE)
630    CALL HCHAR(PROW(L),PCOLUMN(L),CODE)
640    FOR T=1 TO 50
650    NEXT T
660    CODE=NEXTCODE
670    NEXT L
680    CALL HCHAR(PROW(1),PCOLUMN(1),CODE)
690    GOTO 500
790    REM ROTATE SQUARE Q
800    CALL GCHAR(QROW(1),QCOLUMN(1),CODE)
810    FOR L=2 TO 16
820    CALL GCHAR(QROW(L),QCOLUMN(L),NEXTCODE)
830    CALL HCHAR(QROW(L),QCOLUMN(L),CODE)
840    FOR T=1 TO 50
850    NEXT T
860    CODE=NEXTCODE
870    NEXT L
880    CALL HCHAR(QROW(1),QCOLUMN(1),CODE)
890    GOTO 500
```

Fig. 5.12. Listing of puzzle program.

Summary

We have developed a number of methods in this chapter for filling the screen with tiling patterns. These patterns were inspired by ideas from geometry and from Islamic art. Some of them can be produced in unexpected ways and some are surprisingly complex. After this a much simpler pattern was created and a technique for making it move was developed. This was the prelude to writing a program for an intriguing puzzle.

Chapter Six
Writing A Game

In this chapter, we shall write a program for a scaled-down Space Invader type of game. The program is restricted to a mini-version of Space Invaders to keep the programming task to a reasonable size so that we can finish having written a fairly short program that can be understood without difficulty while providing a reasonably entertaining game. Having understood the core of the game, the reader can then extend it in any of a number of ways.

It must be admitted at the outset that all arcade games are written in machine code and not in BASIC. The main reason for this is to make the action in the games happen quickly. As soon as a BASIC program assumes any complexity, the action it provides takes place slowly. This is another reason for keeping the game developed here quite simple. Nevertheless, the outline presented for the game is just as suitable for programming in machine code as it is in BASIC.

Our program starts by displaying six Invaders on the screen. They move across it in fairly unpredictable fashion. The user has a firing position which can be moved to the left or to the right, and from which missiles can be launched to shoot down the Invaders. The game terminates naturally when all the Invaders have been despatched.

Obvious ways of extending the game from the stage developed here include designing different Invaders, adding more Invaders and giving them the ability to fire at and destroy the user's missile launcher.

Even with the game in its simple form, there are quite a lot of tasks for the program to perform. These include plotting the Invaders, moving them, scanning the keyboard to see if a command for moving the firing position or for launching a missile has been issued, and responding to these commands when they are given. The commands that the program must recognise are issued by pressing a single key as follows:

KEY	Action
L	Move the firing position to the left
R	Move the firing position to the right
F	Fire a missile

If any other key is pressed it is to be ignored. The keys to be pressed to issue the commands can be changed quite simply if other keys seem to be more convenient.

When a missile is fired, the program must determine whether an Invader is shot down or whether the missile has passed harmlessly off the screen. Furthermore, some activities must appear to take place simultaneously. They cannot actually take place at the same time, of course, since the computer only has a single processor which executes instructions sequentially. The illusion, for example, of moving a missile and the Invaders at the same time is created by moving the missile a little, then moving the Invaders a little, and repeating this for as long as necessary.

Figure 6.1 gives a specification of the actions to be taken by the program in the form of a *flowchart*. This is quite a good way to represent a fairly complex application, and shows how it is broken down into tasks. In the flowchart ordinary computational tasks are enclosed by a rectangular box, points at which a decision must be made are enclosed by a diamond, and a rhombus encloses any task the purpose of which is to provide an output for display.

The initialisation stage can be broken down into the following sub-tasks

1. Represent the Invaders.
2. Design the characters for the Invaders.
3. Clear the screen.
4. Plot the Invaders.
5. Design missile and missile launcher.
6. Plot the missile launcher.
7. Set score to zero.
8. Display score.

To be able to display an Invader we need to know its position, that is, the row and the column that it occupies on the screen, and its code. When an Invader is represented by these three things (row, column and code) it can be displayed using HCHAR. Since we have

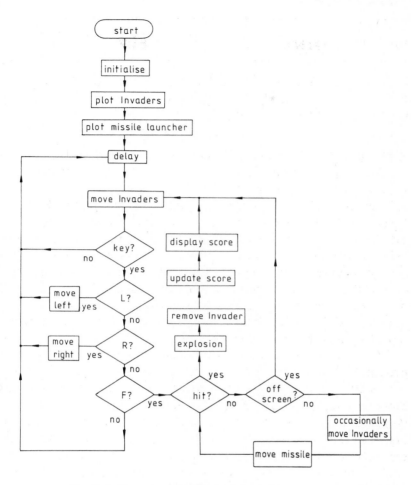

Fig. 6.1. Flowchart for Space Invader game.

six Invaders to deal with, it is convenient to be able to handle them all in the same way. For this reason we shall make use of the *array*. An array is a set of variables which can be used in the same way as ordinary variables, but with the added convenience that they include a bracketed index. An array with six elements can be declared with the statement:

DIM INVADER(6)

This provides us with the six variables INVADER(1) to INVADER(6). (It also gives us INVADER(0), but we shall ignore this. It can be eliminated by using the command OPTION BASE 1.) These variables can be used in the same way as ordinary variables, so that we can set INVADER(1) to 128, INVADER(2) to 129 and so on up to setting INVADER(6) to 133 by:

```
INVADER(1) = 128
INVADER(2) = 129

...

INVADER(6) = 133
```

However, by making use of the bracketed index, it is much easier to set these values with:

```
FOR K = 1 TO 6
INVADER (K) = 127 + K
NEXT K
```

By using six-element arrays to hold the rows, columns and codes for the six Invaders, they can be plotted and moved quite easily. If we use IROW, ICOLUMN and INVADER, respectively, for the rows, columns and codes then they can be declared by:

```
DIM IROW(6), ICOLUMN(6), INVADER(6)
```

Initial positions and codes can be assigned by

```
FOR K = 1 TO 6
IROW(K) = 2 + K
ICOLUMN(K) = 5*K
INVADER(K) = 127 + K
NEXT K
```

Since codes 128 to 133 are being used for the Invaders, we need to design the shapes to go with these codes. In the program the shape description "183C7EDB7E244281" is assigned to codes 128 to 130 and "3C42E75A5A81C366" to codes 131 to 133 using CALL CHAR. The Invaders can then be plotted in their initial positions by:

```
FOR K = 1 TO 6
CALL HCHAR (IROW(K), ICOLUMN(K), INVADER(K))
NEXT K
```

In similar fashion, the Invaders can be moved (to the right) by blanking them out, with a space, increasing their column position by one and then replotting them. After an Invader has reached the position at the extreme right of a row it is moved to the left of the next row down the screen. This can be done by:

```
5000    FOR K=1 TO 6
5010    CALL HCHAR(IROW(K),ICOLUMN(K),32)
5020    ICOLUMN(K)=ICOLUMN(K)+1
5030    IF ICOLUMN(K) <= 32 THEN 5060
5040    IROW(K)=IROW(K)+1
5050    ICOLUMN(K)=1
5060    CALL HCHAR(IROW(K),ICOLUMN(K),INVADER(K))
5070    NEXT K
5080    RETURN
```

The missile launcher and the missile are given codes 136 and 137, and the initial position of the launcher is stored with its row in FROW and its column in FCOLUMN. The plotting and movement of the missile launcher are then achieved in the same way as for an Invader. When a missile is launched, it proceeds up the column occupied by the launcher when it was fired until it hits an Invader or leaves the screen. The score is displayed at the top left of the screen using the subroutine developed in Chapter 2.

In the main part of the program, the keyboard is scanned using the CALL KEY statement. Note that if keys other than R, L and F are thought to be more convenient for moving the missile launcher and for firing missiles, lines 490 to 510 can be modified very easily to enable other keys to be used. The random movement of the Invaders is created by using the random number generator, RND. When RND is used, a random number that is greater than or equal to zero but less than one is generated. Thus a random number in this range can be assigned to the variable R by:

R = RND

The random numbers are generated sequentially each time RND is used. The sequence of random numbers is the same each time the program is run unless the RANDOMIZE statement appears in the program, in which case the sequence varies from run to run. The random numbers are also equally distributed between zero and one. For this reason, if we want an event to occur at random, but to occur *on average* half of the time that every other event within a loop occurs, we can achieve this if the occurrences of the event are controlled by

IF RND <0.5 THEN

Similarly, an event can be made to occur with one tenth of the frequency of others when its occurrences are controlled by:

IF RND <0.1 THEN

This device is used to ensure that the Invaders move, on average, one place across the screen for every ten places moved by a missile fired up the screen at them.

An 'explosion' character is defined to have code 144. It is for use when a missile knocks out an Invader. The explosion character is made to flash by changing the colours assigned to it using CALL COLOR statements. When an Invader is hit, the code for the space character is placed in the appropriate element of the INVADER array to ensure that the destroyed Invader is no longer plotted.

Because the tasks of displaying the score, creating a delay and moving the Invaders are frequently required, and are needed in more than one branch of the program, they are written as subroutines.

The entire program is listed below in Figure 6.2. The special characters defined in the program are listed in the following Table 6.1, and the variables used by the program with their purposes are given in Table 6.2.

Table 6.1. Special characters defined in the Space Invader program.

Code	Character
128	
129	Space Invader 1
130	
131	
132	Space Invader 2
133	
136	Missile launcher
137	Missile
144	Explosion

Table 6.2. Variables used in Space Invader program and their purposes.

Variable	Purpose of Variable
A$	Holds shape description of Invader 1.
B$	Holds shape description of Invader 2.
CHA	Code of character in next position in missile path.
CODE	Code returned by CALL KEY.
DELAY	Variable in delay loop.
FCOLUMN	Column occupied by missile launcher.
FROW	Row occupied by missile launcher.
ICOLUMN	Array for columns occupied by Invaders.
INVADER	Array for codes of Invaders.
IROW	Array for rows occupied by Invaders.
MROW	Row for missile path.
SCORE	Score of Invaders destroyed.
STATUS	Status of CALL KEY.

```
100    REM SIMPLE SPACE INVADERS
110    REM *** INITIALISATION ***
120    RANDOMIZE
130    DIM IROW(6),ICOLUMN(6),INVADER(6)
140    FOR K=1 TO 6
150    IROW(K)=2+K
160    ICOLUMN(K)=5*K
170    INVADER(K)=127+K
180    NEXT K
190    A$="183C7EDB7E244281"
200    CALL CHAR(128, A$)
210    CALL CHAR(129, A$)
220    CALL CHAR(130, A$)
230    B$="3C42E75A5A81C366"
240    CALL CHAR(131, B$)
250    CALL CHAR(132, B$)
260    CALL CHAR(133, B$)
270    CALL CLEAR
280    REM PLOT INVADERS
290    FOR K=1 TO 6
300    CALL HCHAR(IROW(K),ICOLUMN(K),INVADER(K))
310    NEXT K
320    REM DESIGN AND PLOT MISSILE LAUNCHER
330    CALL CHAR(136, "08081C1C3E3EFFFF")
340    CALL CHAR(137, "1818181818181818")
350    CALL COLOR(14, 14, 1)
```

```
360    FROW=24
370    FCOLUMN=16
380    CALL HCHAR(FROW,FCOLUMN,136)
390    CALL CHAR(144, "8142241818244281")
400    CALL COLOR(15, 14, 1)
410    SCORE=0
420    GOSUB 3000
430    GOSUB 4000
440    GOSUB 5000
450    REM *** MAIN PROGRAM LOOPS ***
460    REM SCAN KEYBOARD
470    CALL KEY(0, CODE, STATUS)
480    IF STATUS=0 THEN 430
490    IF CODE=ASC("R") THEN 1000
500    IF CODE=ASC("L") THEN 1100
510    IF CODE=ASC("F") THEN 1200
520    GOTO 430
999    REM MOVE LAUNCHER TO RIGHT
1000   IF FCOLUMN=32 THEN 430
1010   CALL HCHAR(FROW,FCOLUMN,32)
1020   FCOLUMN=FCOLUMN+1
1030   CALL HCHAR(FROW,FCOLUMN,136)
1040   GOTO 430
1099   REM MOVE LAUNCHER TO LEFT
1100   IF FCOLUMN=1 THEN 430
1110   CALL HCHAR(FROW,FCOLUMN,32)
1120   FCOLUMN=FCOLUMN-1
1130   CALL HCHAR(FROW,FCOLUMN,136)
1140   GOTO 430
1199   REM FIRE MISSILE
1200   MROW=23
1210   CALL GCHAR(MROW,FCOLUMN,CHA)
1220   IF (CHA > 127)*(CHA < 134) THEN 2000
1230   IF MROW=1 THEN 2200
1240   CALL HCHAR(MROW,FCOLUMN,137)
1250   IF RND > 0.1 THEN 1270
1260   GOSUB 5000
1270   CALL HCHAR(MROW,FCOLUMN,CHA)
1280   MROW=MROW-1
1290   GOTO 1210
1999   REM INVADER DESTROYED
2000   CALL SOUND(1000,220,2,-5,4)
2010   CALL HCHAR(MROW,FCOLUMN,144)
2020   FOR K=1 TO 8
2030   CALL COLOR(15,1,14)
2040   CALL COLOR(15,14,1)
2050   NEXT K
2060   CALL HCHAR(MROW,FCOLUMN,32)
2070   I=CHA-127
2080   INVADER(I)=32
2090   SCORE=SCORE+1
2100   GOSUB 3000
2110   GOTO 440
```

```
2199    REM MISSILE OFF SCREEN
2200    CALL HCHAR(1,FCOLUMN,CHA)
2210    GOTO 440
2998    REM
2999    REM SUBROUTINE TO DISPLAY SCORE
3000    M$=STR$(SCORE)&" INVADERS DESTROYED"
3010    FOR K=1 TO LEN(M$)
3020    CH=ASC(SEG$(M$,K,1))
3030    CALL HCHAR(1,K+2,CH)
3040    NEXT K
3050    RETURN
3998    REM
3999    REM SUBROUTINE FOR DELAY
4000    FOR DELAY=1 TO 200
4010    NEXT DELAY
4020    RETURN
4998    REM
4999    REM SUBROUTINE TO MOVE INVADERS
5000    FOR K=1 TO 6
5010    CALL HCHAR(IROW(K),ICOLUMN(K),32)
5020    ICOLUMN(K)=ICOLUMN(K)+1
5030    IF ICOLUMN(K) <= 32 THEN 5060
5040    IROW(K)=IROW(K)+1
5050    ICOLUMN(K)=1
5060    CALL HCHAR(IROW(K),ICOLUMN(K),INVADER(K))
5070    NEXT K
5080    RETURN
```

Fig. 6.2. Listing of Space Invader program.

Chapter Seven
Writing A Simple Database

A database program is a program with which information can first be stored and can subsequently be retrieved in any of a variety of ways that may suit the user. Clearly database programs have a vast number of applications. These range from keeping the details of a record collection, or keeping the records of the members of a golf club and administering their handicaps to controlling the stock held by a shop. It is possible to purchase any of a large number of database programs for these kinds of purposes. The better ones tend to be rather expensive and, because they are quite generally applicable, they require a certain amount of study before they can be used. For this reason we shall develop in this chapter a simple database program. With its aid the user will have a program, or will be able to proceed to develop one, for use in any simple, or even moderately complex, application requiring data storage and retrieval.

The features of TI BASIC that are introduced in this chapter are those for file handling. These are necessary because the information contained in the database must be stored permanently in some way or else it will have to be entered afresh every time the program is used. This is obviously neither desirable nor practical. Thus, after the information has been entered initially, it is stored in a file on cassette using the file-handling commands. When the information is required subsequently, it can be read from the file on cassette.

The database program

Suppose we are interested in keeping track of the price and capabilities of the various items of software that are available for our computer so that we can decide what to buy when we have some money to spend. The details that we are likely to be interested in for each item of software include its title, price, type and the amount of memory that it requires. If we were keeping this information on record cards to be stored in a card box, rather than as records to be stored in a database, we could design a record card as shown in Figure 7.1 for the purpose. Each card would hold the details of one item of software, and the card box would be full of such cards. If more details are needed, such as what medium the software is available on, then a further field can be added to each card.

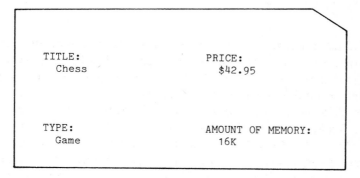

Fig. 7.1. File card.

Once all the information is recorded in this way, we can sort it or search it to obtain particular information that we may require. For example, to find all the items of software of a particular type that are represented in our card box, all we have to do is to examine each card, compare its TYPE field to see if it matches the type we require and to select every card where the match succeeds. A more complicated search might be made for all the software of a particular type that costs less than a certain price. In this case both the TYPE and the PRICE fields of every card must be examined, and the cards to be selected are those for which the entries in both fields match our requirements.

To write our database, we need to store the information in a way analogous to that used with the card file. It can then be searched and examined in ways comparable to those that are used with a card file. One way to store the information so as to allow this is to store it in a set of arrays, with one to hold the titles, one for the prices, one for the types and one for the amounts of memory required. If other details of items of software are to be recorded, then further arrays can be added. In this way, the first record will be stored in the first elements of the arrays, the second record in the second elements and so on.

Note that the titles and types must be stored in arrays of string variables while the prices and amounts of memory required can be stored in arrays of numeric variables. If we assume that the price is always given in pounds and the amount of memory required in kilobytes, then we could write assignments to store the information represented in Figure 7.1 as the first record in the database. The assignments are:

```
TITLE$(1) = "CHESS"
PRICE(1) = 42.95
TYPE$(1) = "GAME"
MEMORY(1) = 16
```

In practice, of course, we shall enter all the information using a FOR...NEXT loop. If we use INPUT statements, and assume that the database contains twenty records, then the information can be entered and accepted by the following statements:

```
DIM TITLE$(20), PRICE(20), TYPE$(20),
    MEMORY(20)
FOR K = 1 TO 20
DISPLAY "ENTER RECORD", K
INPUT "TITLE:" : TITLE$(K)
INPUT "PRICE:" : PRICE(K)
INPUT "TYPE:":TYPE$(K)
INPUT "MEMORY:" : MEMORY(K)
NEXT K
```

This way of entering information is rather dull, at least in terms of the screen display produced, compared to that introduced in Chapter 3. It is used in the database program to illustrate an alternative means of data entry. The reader may care to improve the way in which the program accepts its inputs by adapting the techniques from Chapter 3.

Once the information has all been entered and stored in the arrays it must be stored in some permanent way or it will be lost when the computer is turned off. We shall do this by storing it in a file on cassette unit number one. (It is equally easy to store it on cassette unit number two or on any other storage medium such as disk provided the necessary storage unit is attached to the computer.) This can be done by opening a file and associating cassette unit number one with the file. Subsequently, the data can be written to the file by using the PRINT# statement together with the file number. The information can be copied from the arrays to the file by:

```
OPEN#1: "CS1", OUTPUT, INTERNAL, SEQUENTIAL,
   FIXED
FOR K = 1 TO 20
PRINT#1: TITLE$(K), PRICE(K), TYPE$(K), MEMORY(K)
NEXT K
CLOSE#1
```

The file is opened as file number one (any number from 1 to 255 could have been chosen). Because it is opened for output it can only be written to. As explained more fully in the User's Reference Guide, the records are written in the computer's INTERNAL form, SEQUENTIALly, and as records of FIXED length since all our records have the same format.

When the data has been placed in a file in this way, it can be read back into the arrays in the main program by:

```
OPEN#2: "CS1", INPUT, INTERNAL, SEQUENTIAL,
   FIXED
FOR K = 1 TO 20
INPUT#2: TITLE$(K), PRICE(K), TYPE$(K), MEMORY(K)
NEXT K
CLOSE#2
```

This time the file on cassette unit number one should be opened for input. In this way its contents can be read into the computer. They are transferred sequentially using INPUT# statements with the number assigned to the file.

Using these methods, we can fill the arrays in the main program with the necessary information whether the information is entered at the keyboard or stored in a file. The information can then be searched, for example, for all items of software classified as games by:

```
10 FOR K = 1 TO 20
20 IF TYPE$(K) = "GAME" THEN 30 ELSE 40
30 DISPLAY TITLE$(K)
40 NEXT K
```

The equivalents of OR and AND for use in logical expressions that are developed in Chapter 3 are particularly useful if our search criterion involves more than one field. To illustrate this, we can find all the items of software that are games and cost less than £50 with:

```
10 FOR K = 1 TO 20
20 IF (TYPE$(K) = "GAME")*(PRICE(K)<50) THEN 30
```

```
        ELSE 40
   30 DISPLAY TITLE$(K)
   40 NEXT K
```

Structure of the database program

The structure of the database program is shown in Figure 7.2. The

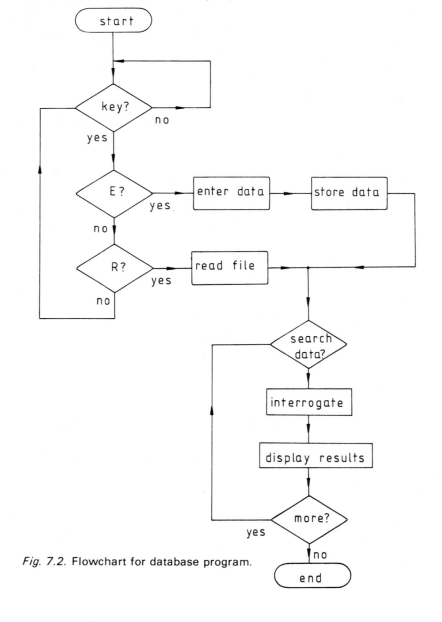

Fig. 7.2. Flowchart for database program.

program starts by asking the user if the data is to be entered from the keyboard or from a file and it then takes the appropriate action. The database can then be interrogated. The simple form of interrogation that is implemented involves searching the database on one field looking for matches to a given pattern. In this way the database can be searched for items of software of a particular type, of a given price or needing a specified amount of storage.

When the information is entered from the keyboard the program provides the user with the chance to correct it if it is not entered correctly. Note that the computer itself generates the messages instructing the user to operate the cassette unit. The complete database program is shown in Figure 7.3 below.

```
100    REM DATABASE PROGRAM
110    REM *** DATA ENTRY ***
120    DIM TITLE$(20),PRICE(20),TYPE$(20),MEMORY(20)
130    CALL CLEAR
140    DISPLAY "      DATA ENTRY"
150    DISPLAY "FOR ENTRY FROM KEYBOARD-PRESS K"
160    DISPLAY "FOR ENTRY FROM FILE-PRESS F"
170    CALL KEY(0, CODE, STATUS)
180    IF STATUS=0 THEN 170
190    IF CODE=ASC("K") THEN 300
200    IF CODE=ASC("F") THEN 500
210    GOTO 170
299    REM ENTRY FROM KEYBOARD
300    FOR K=1 TO 20
310    DISPLAY "ENTER RECORD", K
320    INPUT "TITLE:": TITLE$(K)
330    INPUT "PRICE:" : PRICE(K)
340    INPUT "TYPE:": TYPE$(K)
350    INPUT "MEMORY:": MEMORY(K)
360    DISPLAY "PRESS A TO ACCEPT THIS DATA"
370    DISPLAY "PRESS ANY OTHER KEY TO RE-ENTER"
380    CALL KEY(0, CODE, STATUS)
390    IF STATUS=0 THEN 380
400    IF CODE <> ASC("A") THEN 310
410    NEXT K
420    OPEN #1: "CS1",OUTPUT,INTERNAL,SEQUENTIAL,FIXED
430    FOR K=1 TO 20
440    PRINT #1: TITLE$(K),PRICE(K),TYPE$(K),MEMORY(K)
450    NEXT K
460    CLOSE #1
470    GOTO 600
499    REM ENTRY FROM FILE
500    OPEN #2: "CS1",INPUT,INTERNAL,SEQUENTIAL,FIXED
510    FOR K=1 TO 20
520    INPUT #2: TITLE$(K),PRICE(K),TYPE$(K),MEMORY(K)
530    NEXT K
```

```
540     CLOSE #2
599     REM *** INTERROGATION ***
600     CALL CLEAR
610     DISPLAY "INTERROGATION"
620     DISPLAY " PRESS 1 FOR PRICE"
630     DISPLAY "       2 FOR TYPE"
640     DISPLAY "       3 FOR MEMORY"
650     CALL KEY(0, CODE, STATUS)
660     IF STATUS=0 THEN 650
670     IF CODE=ASC("1") THEN 750
680     IF CODE=ASC("2") THEN 850
690     IF CODE=ASC("3") THEN 950
700     GOTO 650
750     DISPLAY "ENTER PRICE REQUIRED"
760     INPUT P
770     FOR K=1 TO 20
780     IF PRICE=P THEN 790 ELSE 800
790     DISPLAY TITLE$(K)
800     NEXT K
810     GOTO 1010
850     DISPLAY "ENTER TYPE REQUIRED"
860     INPUT T$
870     FOR K=1 TO 20
880     IF TYPE$(K)=T$ THEN 890 ELSE 900
890     DISPLAY TITLE$(K)
900     NEXT K
910     GOTO 1010
950     DISPLAY "ENTER AMOUNT OF MEMORY REQUIRED"
960     INPUT M
970     FOR K=1 TO 20
980     IF MEMORY=M THEN 990 ELSE 1000
990     DISPLAY TITLE$(K)
1000    NEXT K
1010    DISPLAY "PRESS SPACE FOR FURTHER INTERROGATION"
1020    DISPLAY "AND ANY OTHER KEY TO END"
1030    CALL KEY (0, CODE, STATUS)
1040    IF STATUS=0 THEN 1030
1050    IF CODE=32 THEN 600
1060    END
```

Fig. 7.3. Listing of database program.

Chapter Eight
Writing A Simulation

Simulation is a valuable application for computers in many areas. In industry it is used to test the integrity of a complex system such as an aeroplane without incurring the expense involved in actually constructing the system. An administration can use it to test the effectiveness of new administrative procedures, for purposes such as controlling the flow of traffic, without risking the chaos that might result from putting them into practice straight away.

In this chapter we shall develop a simulation of a tank moving around a fixed path composed of roads and tracks. At certain points the path divides so that the tank driver must decide whether to turn to the right or the left. The simulation is to be written so that commands can be issued while it is in progress by pressing a single key. With the commands that are available we can direct the tank as to which way it should turn at a junction in the path, we can cause an obstacle to be placed in the path of the tank at a random position along the path, and we can decide whether or not the tank should have the capability to avoid automatically any obstacle in its path. Messages are displayed at the top of the screen to indicate the current status of the simulation with regard to each of the three factors over which the user has control.

The layout of the path to be followed by the tank is shown in Figure 8.1. The path is displayed by placing specially designed characters in each of 106 screen locations. The characters that are specially designed for plotting the path are assigned the codes 128 to 135. The characters with codes 128 and 129 are, respectively, horizontal and vertical line characters for plotting the horizontal and vertical sections of the path. The characters with codes 130 to 133 provide the rounded corners, and those with codes 134 and 135 provide the points at which the path divides into two or at which two paths converge. Since the tank must always move along the paths in the directions indicated by the arrows in Figure 8.1, the path only

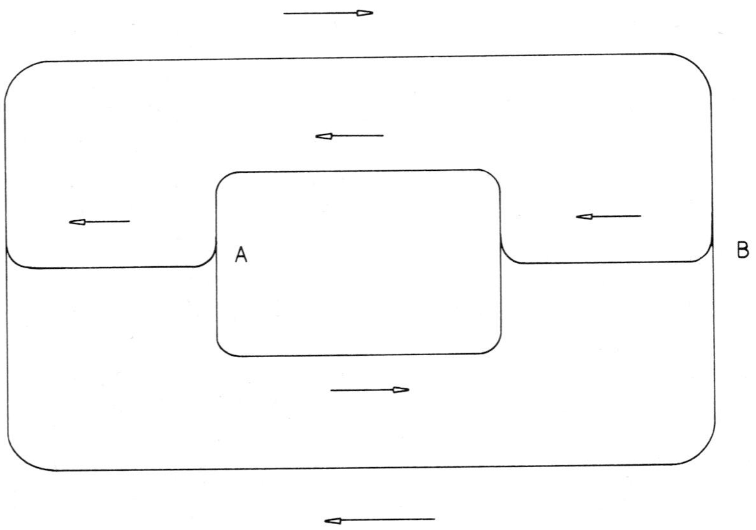

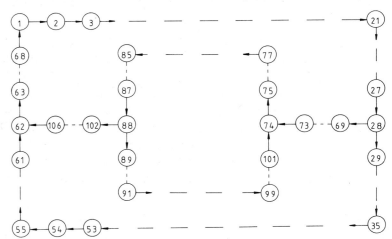

Fig. 8.1. Layout of path.

divides at the points labelled A and B in the figure. It is at these points that the tank driver must decide which way to turn. The 106 screen locations to be occupied by the graphics characters making up the path are placed and labelled as indicated in Figure 8.2. Each location can, as usual, be fixed by giving its row and column, and the positions of all the screen locations on the tank's path are stored in the 106-element arrays named ROW and COLUMN.

When the ROW and COLUMN arrays are initialised and the

Fig. 8.2. The locations on the path and their connections.

characters for plotting the track are defined, the path can be plotted by:

```
CALL HCHAR (ROW (1), COLUMN (1), 128, 21)
CALL HCHAR (ROW (55), COLUMN (55), 128, 21)
CALL HCHAR (ROW (85), COLUMN (85), 128, 9)
CALL HCHAR (ROW (91), COLUMN (91), 128, 9)
CALL VCHAR (ROW (1), COLUMN (1), 129, 15)
CALL VCHAR (ROW (21), COLUMN (21), 129, 15)
CALL VCHAR (ROW (85), COLUMN (85), 129, 7)
CALL VCHAR (ROW (77), COLUMN (77), 129, 7)
CALL HCHAR (ROW (62), COLUMN (62), 128, 7)
CALL HCHAR (ROW (74), COLUMN (74), 128, 7)
CALL HCHAR (ROW (1), COLUMN (1), 131)
CALL HCHAR (ROW (21), COLUMN (21), 130)
CALL HCHAR (ROW (35), COLUMN (35), 132)
CALL HCHAR (ROW (55), COLUMN (55), 133)
CALL HCHAR (ROW (62), COLUMN (62), 134)
CALL HCHAR (ROW (88), COLUMN (88), 135)
CALL HCHAR (ROW (74), COLUMN (74), 134)
CALL HCHAR (ROW (28), COLUMN (28), 135)
```

To display the tank we shall use the special character designed in Chapter 2, assigning it the code 144. The position of the tank on its path is held in the variable TANKPOS. Once TANKPOS is initialised, the tank can be plotted by:

```
CALL HCHAR (ROW(TANKPOS), COLUMN(TANKPOS),
    144)
```

However, to make the tank move along its path we always need to know the position after the present one to which the tank will move next. Thus, the position after position 1 is position 2, and that after position 2 is position 3. But, as Figure 8.2 shows, the next position is not always given by increasing the current position number by one. In particular, the position after position 68 is position 1, while the position following number 28 may be either 29 or 69 depending on which way the tank turns at point B. To record the position after each position on the path, we use the array named AFTER, so that, for example:

AFTER (68) = 1

and

AFTER (106) = 62

When this array is initialised, the tank can be moved along its path in such a way that the plotted path is not destroyed by repeatedly executing

> CALL HCHAR (ROW (TANKPOS), COLUMN (TANKPOS),
>   TEMP)
> TANKPOS = AFTER (TANKPOS)
> CALL GCHAR (ROW (TANKPOS), COLUMN (TANKPOS),
>   TEMP)
> CALL HCHAR (ROW (TANKPOS), COLUMN (TANKPOS),
>   144)

(We can note in passing that it would be more helpful to call the array of next positions NEXT rather than AFTER, since TANKPOS = NEXT(TANKPOS) is more readily understood than TANKPOS = AFTER (TANKPOS). Unfortunately, NEXT is a *reserved word* in TI BASIC, being reserved for use in FOR...NEXT loops, and so cannot be used as a variable name.)

Messages are placed on the screen to show the status of the simulation. They are placed above the tank track and are positioned using our standard display subroutine from Chapter 3.

The keys listed in the following Table 8.1 are used to issue the interactive commands.

Table 8.1. Keys and commands for simulation.

Key	Command
T	Change direction in which tank turns at a branch in the path from right to left or from left to right.
O	Generate an obstacle if none exists, or remove an obstacle if one exists.
A	Activate or deactivate automatic avoidance of obstacles.

In essence there are three aspects of the simulation each of which can assume one of two states. These states are initialised at the beginning of the simulation, but every time a command is issued the relevant aspect is switched from one of its states to the other. The state of each aspect is always recorded by the messages at the top of the screen.

One aspect is the direction in which a tank turns when it comes to a branch in the path at A or B in Figure 8.1. It is initialised to turn to the left and will contine to do so until the T command is issued when it will consistently turn to the right. Each time this command is given the turning status of the tank is altered. The turning status is recorded in the variable TURN. Assigning it a value of 1 represents turning to the right, and zero represents turning to the left. Each time this command is issued we must cause the appropriate message to be displayed and also amend the AFTER array. At point B, if the tank is to turn to the left we must have:

AFTER (28) = 29

whereas if it is to turn to the right we require

AFTER (28) = 69

These changes must be made every time the turning command is issued. The value of the variable TURN can be altered as is appropriate by:

```
10 IF TURN = 1 THEN 40
20 TURN = 1
30 GOTO 50
40 TURN = 0
50
```

or, much more compactly, by:

TURN = 1 − TURN

The O command is used to create an obstacle on the path if none exists currently. The random number function is used to generate a random position for the obstacle. The obstacle itself is assigned the code 136. If the tank should strike the obstacle it will be destroyed. If this command is issued when an obstacle is already on the path, then it will cause the obstacle to be removed. The obstacle status is recorded in the variable OBSTACLE, with a value of zero representing no obstacle and a non-zero value representing not only the existence of an obstacle but also its position on the path.

The third command is issued with the A key and affects the ability of the tank automatically to avoid any obstacle in its path. If this capability is not assigned currently, then issuing the command assigns it and vice versa. If the tank's capability for avoiding an obstacle is switched off then it inevitably crashes into any obstacle on the track but if the capability is turned on it automatically invokes a procedure for skirting round the obstacle. The automatic avoidance status is recorded in the variable AVOID with zero indicating its absence and one its presence.

Program specification

A specification of the simulation program based on the preceding somewhat informal discussion may be written as follows:

    Initialise path
    Initialise tank
    Initialise variables
    Clear the screen
    Display status messages
    Plot path
    Plot tank
    Repeatedly
        Examine next position
        IF obstacle there   THEN
            IF avoidance on   THEN avoid it ELSE crash
                                ELSE
        Move tank
        Scan keyboard
        IF command issued THEN obey it ELSE delav

The flowchart given in Figure 8.3 expands and refines this description of the program.

At this stage, the only task of any particular difficulty is that of programming the tank to avoid obstacles automatically. On closer inspection this task is not too severe as it resolves itself into the two cases, represented in Figure 8.4, of avoiding an obstacle along a straight path or of avoiding it when it is on a corner. In the figure, the current position of the tank is indicated by TANKPOS, the position of the obstacle by OBSTACLE and the destination of the tank after it has avoided the obstacle by DESTINATION. The test to see if there is an obstacle in the next position is given by:

    IF AFTER (TANKPOS) = OBSTACLE THEN ...

DESTINATION is given by

    DESTINATION = AFTER (AFTER (TANKPOS))

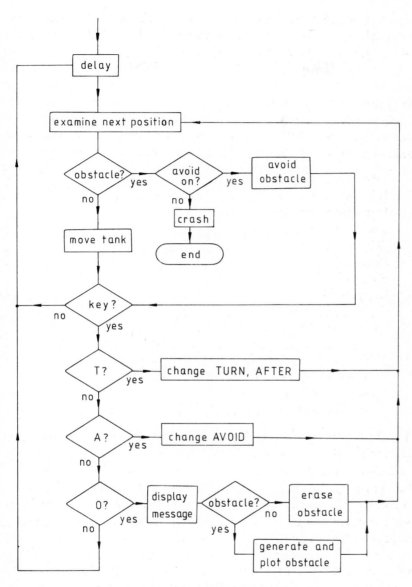

Fig. 8.3. Flowchart for simulation program.

Fig. 8.4. Avoiding obstacles.

or, equally well, by

DESTINATION = AFTER (OBSTACLE)

The paths for avoiding the obstacle are indicated in Figure 8.4 by broken lines. Avoidance on a straight line path involves visiting three screen positions that are off the tank's path, but if the obstacle is on a corner the tank can cut the corner and need only visit one screen location away from the path. In fact, because the simulation program is getting rather long, the program presented here only allows obstacles to fall on the top and bottom horizontal sections of the path. This simplifies the avoidance procedure considerably. However, we shall discuss the general avoidance procedure a little further to help you implement it for yourself should you wish to do so.

The key to determining how to avoid an obstacle automatically is to find the pattern of the positions occupied by the three positions TANKPOS, OBSTACLE and DESTINATION. If they lie on a horizontal straight line the tank can skip round the obstacle by taking three positions above the path as in Figure 8.4(a). If they lie on a vertical straight line the tank can take three positions to the right of the path, and if the obstacle is on a corner, the tank can cut the corner as shown in Figure 8.4(b).

The pattern of positions can be found by using a test such as:

IF ROW (TANKPOS) = ROW (OBSTACLE) THEN ...
ELSE

If the test is true then the tank and the obstacle are in the same row, but if the test is false they are in the same column. Making successively the tests for whether

ROW (TANKPOS) = ROW (OBSTACLE)

and for whether

ROW (OBSTACLE) = ROW (DESTINATION)

will give the pattern of the three positions. If both tests are true they are all in a row, and if both tests are false they are all in a column. When one is true and the other is false the obstacle is on a corner. In this case, if the first test is true the tank is approaching the corner on a horizontal part of the path and if it is false the tank approaches on a vertical part. This is summarised in Figure 8.5, and inspection of this figure shows, for example, that the location of the position for cutting the corner when the first test is true and the second is false has its row given by ROW (DESTINATION) and its column by

TEST 1 ROW(TANKPOS)= ROW(OBSTACLE)?	TEST 2 ROW(OBSTACLE)= ROW(DESTINATION)?	CONFIGURATION
TRUE	TRUE	
TRUE	FALSE	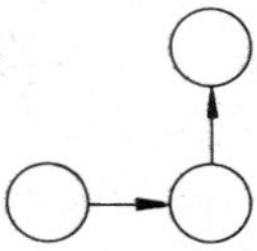
FALSE	TRUE	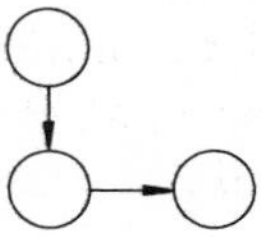
FALSE	FALSE	

Fig. 8.5. Patterns of the positions for avoidance.

COLUMN (TANKPOS) so that we can plot the tank cutting the corner with:

   CALL HCHAR (ROW (DESTINATION), COLUMN (TANKPOS), 144)

The entire interactive simulation program can now be written. It is listed below in Figure 8.6. The following Tables 8.2 and 8.3 give, respectively, the codes for the special characters defined in the program and the variables used by the program with their purposes.

Table 8.2. Special characters defined in the simulation program.

Code	Character
128	Horizontal character for path
129	Vertical character for path
130	
131	
132	Corner characters for path
133	
134	
135	Branching characters for path
136	Obstacle
144	Tank

Table 8.3. Variables used in simulation program and their purposes.

Variable	Purpose of variable
AFTER	Array of next positions on path
AVOID	Records whether automatic avoidance of obstacles is on or off
CODE	Code returned by CALL KEY
COLUMN	Array holding columns for path positions
DESTINATION	Position of tank on path after avoiding an obstacle
M$	Holds messages for display
MCOLUMN	Gives column in which message starts
MROW	Gives row in which message starts
OBSTACLE	Gives position of obstacle or is zero for no obstacle
ROW	Array holding rows for path positions
STATUS	Status of CALL KEY
TANKPOS	Holds position of tank
TEMP	Holds code for path character in position occupied by tank
TURN	Records turning state of tank

```
100   REM TANK SIMULATION
110   REM *** INITIALISATION ***
120   DIM ROW(106), COLUMN(106), AFTER(106)
130   FOR K=1 TO 21
140   ROW(K)=8
150   COLUMN(K)=5+K
160   NEXT K
170   FOR K=22 TO 34
180   ROW(K)=K-13
190   COLUMN(K)=26
200   NEXT K
210   FOR K=35 TO 55
220   ROW(K)=22
230   COLUMN(K)=61-K
240   NEXT K
250   FOR K=56 TO 68
260   ROW(K)=77-K
270   COLUMN(K)=6
280   NEXT K
290   FOR K=69 TO 74
300   ROW(K)=15
310   COLUMN(K)=94-K
320   NEXT K
330   ROW(75)=14
340   COLUMN(75)=20
350   ROW(76)=13
360   COLUMN(76)=20
370   FOR K=77 TO 85
380   ROW(K)=12
390   COLUMN(K)=97-K
400   NEXT K
410   FOR K=86 TO 90
420   ROW(K)=K-73
430   COLUMN(K)=12
440   NEXT K
450   FOR K=91 TO 99
460   ROW(K)=18
470   COLUMN(K)=K-79
480   NEXT K
490   ROW(100)=17
500   COLUMN(100)=20
510   ROW(101)=16
520   COLUMN(101)=20
530   FOR K=102 TO 106
540   ROW(K)=15
550   COLUMN(K)=113-K
560   NEXT K
570   CALL CHAR(128, "000000FF")
580   CALL CHAR(129, "0808080808080808")
590   CALL CHAR(130, "000000C020100808")
600   CALL CHAR(131, "0000000102040408")
610   CALL CHAR(132, "081020C0")
620   CALL CHAR(133, "08040201")
```

```
630    CALL CHAR(134, "080C0A0908080808")
640    CALL CHAR(135, "1828488808080808")
650    CALL CHAR(136, "FFFFC3C3FFFFFFFF")
660    FOR K=1 TO 105
670    AFTER(K)=K+1
680    NEXT K
690    AFTER(68)=1
700    AFTER(106)=63
710    CALL CHAR(144, "10387F78307CAA7C")
720    TANKPOS=1
730    AVOID=0
740    OBSTACLE=0
750    TURN=0
760    CALL CLEAR
770    REM MESSAGES
780    M$="TURN TO LEFT "
790    MROW=1
800    MCOLUMN=3
810    GOSUB 2000
820    M$="NO OBSTACLE ON TRACK"
830    MROW=3
840    MCOLUMN=3
850    GOSUB 2000
860    M$="AUTOMATIC AVOIDANCE OFF"
870    MROW=2
880    MCOLUMN=16
890    GOSUB 2000
900    GOSUB 3000
910    CALL GCHAR(ROW(TANKPOS),COLUMN(TANKPOS),TEMP)
920    CALL HCHAR(ROW(TANKPOS),COLUMN(TANKPOS),144)
930    GOSUB 4000
999    REM *** MAIN SECTION OF PROGRAM ***
1000   CALL HCHAR(ROW(TANKPOS),COLUMN(TANKPOS),TEMP)
1010   IF AFTER(TANKPOS)=OBSTACLE THEN 1060 ELSE 1020
1020   TANKPOS=AFTER(TANKPOS)
1030   CALL GCHAR(ROW(TANKPOS),COLUMN(TANKPOS),TEMP)
1040   CALL HCHAR(ROW(TANKPOS),COLUMN(TANKPOS),144)
1050   GOTO 1250
1060   IF AVOID=1 THEN 1070 ELSE 1090
1070   GOSUB 5000
1080   GOTO 1250
1090   CALL SOUND(2000,-5,2)
1100   CALL HCHAR(ROW(TANKPOS),COLUMN(TANKPOS),136)
1110   FOR J=1 TO 8
1120   CALL COLOR(14,1,2)
1130   CALL COLOR(14,2,1)
1140   NEXT J
1150   M$="TANK DESTROYED BY OBSTACLE"
1160   MROW=5
1170   MCOLUMN=3
1180   GOSUB 2000
1190   STOP
1250   CALL KEY(0, CODE, STATUS)
```

```
1260     IF STATUS=0 THEN 930
1270     IF CODE=ASC("T") THEN 1400
1280     IF CODE=ASC("A") THEN 1600
1290     IF CODE=ASC("O") THEN 1800
1300     GOTO 930
1399     REM CHANGES FOR TURN
1400     TURN=1-TURN
1410     MROW=1
1420     MCOLUMN=3
1430     IF TURN=1 THEN 1440 ELSE 1490
1440     M$="TURN TO RIGHT"
1450     GOSUB 2000
1460     AFTER(28)=69
1470     AFTER(88)=102
1480     GOTO 1000
1490     M$="TURN TO LEFT "
1500     GOSUB 2000
1510     AFTER(28)=29
1520     AFTER(88)=89
1530     GOTO 1000
1599     REM CHANGES FOR AVOID
1600     AVOID=1-AVOID
1610     MROW=2
1620     MCOLUMN=16
1630     IF AVOID=1 THEN 1640 ELSE 1670
1640     M$="AUTOMATIC AVOIDANCE ON "
1650     GOSUB 2000
1660     GOTO 1000
1670     M$="AUTOMATIC AVOIDANCE OFF"
1680     GOSUB 2000
1690     GOTO 1000
1799     REM CHANGES FOR OBSTACLE
1800     MROW=3
1810     MCOLUMN=3
1820     IF OBSTACLE=0 THEN 1830 ELSE 1920
1830     M$="   OBSTACLE ON TRACK"
1840     GOSUB 2000
1850     IF RND < 0.5 THEN 1860 ELSE 1880
1860     OBSTACLE=2+INT(18*RND)
1870     GOTO 1890
1880     OBSTACLE=36+INT(18*RND)
1890     CALL GCHAR(ROW(OBSTACLE),COLUMN(OBSTACLE),TEMP2)
1900     CALL HCHAR(ROW(OBSTACLE),COLUMN(OBSTACLE),136)
1910     GOTO 1000
1920     M$="NO OBSTACLE ON TRACK"
1930     GOSUB 2000
1940     CALL HCHAR(ROW(OBSTACLE),COLUMN(OBSTACLE),TEMP2)
1950     OBSTACLE=0
1960     GOTO 1000
1970     END
1998     REM
1999     REM DISPLAY SUBROUTINE
2000     FOR K=1 TO LEN(M$)
```

```
2010   CH=ASC(SEG$(M$,K,1))
2020   CALL HCHAR(MROW,MCOLUMN-1+K,CH)
2030   NEXTK
2040   RETURN
2998   REM
2999   REM SUBROUTINE TO PLOT TRACK
3000   CALL HCHAR(ROW(1),COLUMN(1),128,21)
3010   CALL HCHAR(ROW(55),COLUMN(55),128,21)
3020   CALL HCHAR(ROW(85),COLUMN(85),128,9)
3030   CALL HCHAR(ROW(91),COLUMN(91),128,9)
3040   CALL VCHAR(ROW(1),COLUMN(1),129,15)
3050   CALL VCHAR(ROW(21),COLUMN(21),129,15)
3060   CALL VCHAR(ROW(85),COLUMN(85),129,7)
3070   CALL VCHAR(ROW(77),COLUMN(77),129,7)
3080   CALL HCHAR(ROW(62),COLUMN(62),128,7)
3090   CALL HCHAR(ROW(74),COLUMN(74),128,7)
3100   CALL HCHAR(ROW(1),COLUMN(1),131)
3110   CALL HCHAR(ROW(21),COLUMN(21),130)
3120   CALL HCHAR(ROW(35),COLUMN(35),132)
3130   CALL HCHAR(ROW(55),COLUMN(55),133)
3140   CALL HCHAR(ROW(62),COLUMN(62),134)
3150   CALL HCHAR(ROW(88),COLUMN(88),135)
3160   CALL HCHAR(ROW(74),COLUMN(74),134)
3170   CALL HCHAR(ROW(28),COLUMN(28),135)
3180   RETURN
3998   REM
3999   REM DELAY SUBROUTINE
4000   FOR DELAY=1 TO 100
4010   NEXT DELAY
4020   RETURN
4998   REM
4999   REM SUBROUTINE FOR AVOIDING OBSTACLES
5000   DESTINATION=AFTER(OBSTACLE)
5010   R=ROW(TANKPOS)-1
5020   T=TANKPOS
5030   CALL HCHAR(ROW(TANKPOS),COLUMN(TANKPOS),TEMP)
5040   FOR K=1 TO 3
5050   CALL HCHAR(R,COLUMN(T),144)
5060   GOSUB 4000
5070   CALL HCHAR(R,COLUMN(T),32)
5080   T=AFTER(T)
5090   NEXT K
5100   CALL GCHAR(ROW(DESTINATION),COLUMN(DESTINATION),
       TEMP)
5110   CALL HCHAR(ROW(DESTINATION),COLUMN(DESTINATION),
       144)
5120   TANKPOS=DESTINATION
5130   RETURN
```

Fig. 8.6. Listings of simulation program.

Chapter Nine
Expanding The TI99/4A

There is a good deal of both hardware and software with which the TI99/4A can be expanded. This is one of the strengths of the computer. Although the basic machine can be obtained at a modest price, it can be expanded in any of a large number of ways to grow as its owner's interests develop.

The software that is available can be classified broadly into four categories. These are games, educational programs, serious programs and programming languages. The games include such favourites as TI Invaders and Munchman, but there are also many adventure games and even chess. The educational programs typically introduce such topics as reading, grammar and arithmetic. Most of the games and educational software are available conveniently as plug-in modules, although some are also available on cassette. The serious programs include a word processor and a so-called 'personal record keeper'. The programming languages include Extended TI BASIC, LOGO and UCSD Pascal. Many of the serious programs and the languages are also available as plug-in modules, but otherwise the medium is disk. Much of this software is written to take advantage of the hardware that can be added to the computer.

The extra peripherals for the TI99/4A include the speech synthesiser and joysticks. There is also a peripheral expansion unit with the aid of which disk drives, a printer, extra memory and many other facilities can be added to the computer. It is worth mentioning that means of handling many of these peripherals are built into the programming languages that can be used with the computer. For example, there is a CALL JOYST statement in TI BASIC for handling joysticks and, as we shall see, Extended TI BASIC has statements for operating the speech module.

Since the main thrust of this book has been concerned with programming, the remainder of this chapter is devoted to introducing the programming languages Extended TI BASIC and LOGO. Once TI BASIC has been mastered, it is natural to progress to the use of the extended version, which is not only more powerful but also enhances the computer's sound and graphics capabilities considerably. LOGO is a language that is widely advocated for educational use. Whether it allows the computer's potential as an educational aid to be realised or it is seen as an alternative to BASIC, LOGO is a very interesting language that is assuming increasing importance.

Extended TI BASIC

The extended version of BASIC for the TI99/4A is available as a plug-in module. When it is plugged into the computer, it can be chosen from the master selection list. It possesses some features that are improvements on those of TI BASIC and it adds others to them. Altogether, more than forty new or extended features are provided.

The extended features include a DISPLAY AT statement, of the kind that we had to write for ourselves in TI BASIC. With this, information to be displayed can be positioned anywhere on the screen. However, the statement is more powerful than this since it can cause the screen to be cleared before displaying the information and can also cause a tone to be sounded. There are also DISPLAY USING and PRINT USING statements with which the format of the information to be displayed can be specified precisely. The IF...THEN...ELSE statement has been made considerably more powerful. The condition part of the statement can contain any of the logical operators NOT, XOR, AND and OR. Again, this corresponds with something we had to construct for ourselves in TI BASIC. In addition to this the general form of the statement is:

IF condition THEN statement 1 ELSE statement 2

where statement 1 and statement 2 can be any statements or, in fact, even sequences of statements. This conditional statement is very powerful, and it permits many of the infelicities associated with the restricted form of the conditional statement in TI BASIC to be avoided. There are also facilities for error handling which are provided by the CALL ERR statement.

Of the new features, the most attractive and characteristic ones are for producing speech from the speech module and for handling *sprites*. The two statements for generating speech are given in the following Table 9.1.

Table 9.1. The statements for speech generation.

Statement	Result of statement
CALL SAY	To cause the computer to say the words given in a character string or the speech pattern stored in a string variable.
CALL SPGET	To store a speech pattern in a string variable.

In fact, the speech module has a vocabulary of about 400 words and phrases. These are naturally the words that it can be commanded to say, although with some juggling, the words that it possesses can be combined to give others. To illustrate the use of the statements, the computer can be made to say 'I can say things' by

    100 CALL SAY ("I CAN SAY THINGS")

The task is as simple as this because all four words are in the vocabulary. An alternative way to produce the phrase is

    100 CALL SPGET ("I", A$)
    110 CALL SPGET ("CAN", B$)
    120 CALL SPGET ("SAY", C$)
    130 CALL SPGET ("THINGS", D$)
    140 CALL SAY (,A$,,B$,,C$,,D$)

Note the commas in line 140. They must be arranged in this way because the statement expects to be given alternating character strings and string variables.

Thus, to make the computer say anything composed directly from the words in its vocabulary is quite straightforward. New words can be constructed by adding words to each other. For example, 'am' and 'end' can be concatenated to give 'amend' and, because the computer will say numbers as well as words, 'be' and '4' give 'before'. Also, after using SPGET to assign the speech pattern for a word to a string variable, there is some scope for using SEG$ to obtain a part of the speech pattern that gives a particular sound. Endings such as 's' and 'ing' are particularly useful. Unfortunately, this is not as easy as it might seem. We might expect to be able to obtain an 's' sound by storing the speech patterns for 'thing' and 'things' and then removing the former pattern from the latter. However, this idea fails at once when we find that the length of the pattern for 'thing' exceeds that for 'things'!

Before the computer can say anything, it must be presented with a string that starts with characters 96 and 0, and then has a character that gives the number of characters in the following speech pattern followed by the speech pattern itself. The speech pattern can then be spoken by the computer as a result of using CALL SAY. One way to generate random speech patterns and to make the computer 'say' them is illustrated by the next program.

```
100 DISPLAY "ENTER LENGTH OF SPEECH PATTERN"
110 INPUT L
120 A$=CHR$(96)&CHR$(0)&CHR$(L)
130 FOR I=1 TO L
140 R=1+INT(255*RND)
150 A$=A$&CHR$(R)
160 NEXT R
170 CALL SAY(,A$)
180 GOTO 100
```

There are also many statements for *sprite graphics*. A sprite is a graphics character, or a group of characters, that can be made to move. When a sprite is a single graphics character, defined in the way with which we are familiar, by CALL CHAR, the special sprite commands allow it to be positioned, continually moved automatically, magnified, and even to have its shape altered. A sprite can also be defined as a block of four characters. For example, the large tank of Fig. 2.6(b) can be defined as a sprite after using the extended version of the CALL CHAR statement. A string of 64 hexadecimal characters is assigned to a string variable, A$, say, consisting of the 16-character definition of the top left character in the tank, followed by that for the bottom left one and then those of the top right and bottom right characters. The large character can then be assigned a code by, for example, CALL CHAR(100, A$).

The commands that are provided for sprite graphics are given in the following Table 9.2 together with the purposes for which they are intended.

Table 9.2. The statements for sprite graphics.

Command	Purpose of Command
CHAR	To define a character string giving the shape of a sprite.
COINC	To detect coincidences, or collisions, between sprites.
DELSPRITE	To delete a sprite.
DISTANCE	To find the distance between sprites.
LOCATE	To move a sprite to a given position.
MAGNIFY	To magnify sprites.
MOTION	To change the motion of a sprite.
PATTERN	To assign a new shape to a sprite.
POSITION	To return the position of a sprite.
SPRITE	To initialise the shape, position, and motion of a sprite.

It is not difficult to appreciate that these statements make the task of programming games such as Space Invaders and Pacman relatively simple. There are statements for automatically producing movement of, for example, Invaders, for changing their positions and motion so that a degree of unpredictability can be introduced, for detecting when an Invader has been shot down by a missile (another sprite), and for then deleting it. The shape of Pacman can be altered with PATTERN to make him gobble up anything in his path. Realistic animation sequences can also be produced by giving a sprite any of a repertoire of shapes as it moves.

The following short program defines the small tank of Figure 2.6(a) as a sprite, and sets it in motion across the screen, changing its shape as it moves. The two shapes for the tank sprite differ only in the appearance of the tank tracks, and the result of the program is to make the tracks appear to rotate as the tank moves.

```
100 CALL CLEAR
110 CALL CHAR(96, "10387F78307CAA7C")
120 CALL CHAR(100, "10387F78307C547C")
130 CALL COLOR(13,7,7)
140 CALL HCHAR(20,1,128,32)
150 CALL SPRITE (#1,96,5,137,1)
160 CALL MAGNIFY(2)
170 CALL MOTION(#1,0,5)
180 CALL PATTERN(#1,100)
190 FOR DELAY=1 TO 10:: NEXT DELAY
200 CALL PATTERN (#1,96)
210 FOR DELAY=1 TO 10:: NEXT DELAY
220 GOTO 180
```

In Extended TI BASIC, the programmer can write his own named sub-programs using the CALL statement, so that calls to user-written sub-programs can have the same appearance as, for instance, the by now familiar, CALL CLEAR and CALL SPRITE statements. This makes programs much more readable than when they are full of GOSUB statements. The following program illustrates this. It establishes four sprites at the centre of the screen, and starts them in motion, but as soon as they reach a certain distance from the centre of the screen (held in the variable R), they are turned upside down and started back towards the centre again. Their shapes are restored once they come back within range of the centre again. The program is:

```
100 DIM COLOUR(4), RSPEED(4), CSPEED(4)
110 CALL CLEAR
120 CALL CHAR(96, "81423C247E5A4242")
130 CALL CHAR(100, "42425A7E243C4281")
140 FOR S=1 TO 4
150 COLOUR(S)=S+1
160 RSPEED(S)=S-2:: CSPEED(S)=3-S
170 CALL SPRITE (#S,96,COLOUR(S),96,128,
    RSPEED(S),CSPEED(S))
180 NEXT S
190 R=50
200 FOR S=1 TO 4
210 CALL DISTANCE (#S,96,128,D)
220 IF D > R*R THEN CALL CHANGE(S,RSPEED(S),
    CSPEED(S)) ELSE CALL REPLACE(S)
230 NEXT S
240 GOTO 200
250 END
500 SUB CHANGE(S, H, V)
510 CALL PATTERN(#S, 100)
520 H =-H::V=-V
530 CALL MOTION(#S, H, V)
540 FOR DELAY=1 TO 200:: NEXT DELAY
550 SUBEND
600 SUB REPLACE(S)
610 CALL PATTERN(#S,96)
620 SUBEND
```

Note that the sub-programs start with a line having SUB followed by their names and finish with the line SUBEND. Line 220 is very powerful as it allows the program to choose directly between two sub-programs. Because of the length of the delay in the CHANGE sub-program, some of the more slowly moving sprites can be caught at the edge of the region and oscillate there for a time. Altering the length of the delay will change the oscillation effects.

LOGO

LOGO is a language that is highly regarded as a vehicle for accessing the educational potential of the computer. It has the ability to turn the computer into a tool for learning, and for learning by *doing*. The foremost proponent of LOGO is Seymour Papert, and one of his ideas is that with LOGO the computer can be made to provide a 'microworld'. Once established, a microworld can be explored or used as a venue for testing ideas and theories. Because microworlds are restricted, it is comparatively easy to understand what happens in them. The complexity of everyday life is removed. In this way, the LOGO user can learn by programming the computer. This is in distinct contrast to the situation in a good deal of computer-aided education, where the computer programs the learner as, for instance, when it takes him through a series of exercise drills.

The best known of LOGO's microworlds are based on the use of the 'turtle'. The turtle is sometimes a small wheeled vehicle that can be controlled from the computer with commands given in LOGO. In TI LOGO, however, it is a small object on the screen which can be controlled in a similar way. At any time, the turtle occupies a position and faces in some direction. The commands for moving the turtle to another position are FORWARD and BACK, which move it forwards and backwards by a given number of units or turtle steps. To make it turn to the right or the left so that it faces in a different direction, the commands LEFT and RIGHT can be used. The commands PENUP and PENDOWN, which are derived from a floor turtle with a real pen, are applied similarly to a screen turtle and its imaginary pen. They can be used to make the turtle leave a trace, or not, as it moves. With these commands the turtle can be made to follow a square path, drawing a square as it goes, by

```
PENDOWN
FORWARD 100
RIGHT 90
FORWARD 100
RIGHT 90
FORWARD 100
RIGHT 90
FORWARD 100
RIGHT 90
```

This can be abbreviated to

PENDOWN
REPEAT 4 [FORWARD 100 RIGHT 90]

Apart from the turtle commands, LOGO is a complete computer language, and is, in fact, a list processing language. To give a few examples of its capabilities for processing lists, it has features for finding the first item in a list, for removing the first item of a list, for finding the last item of a list, and for removing that from a list. A list is represented by enclosing it in square brackets. Thus:

PRINT FIRST [TEXAS OKLAHOMA ARKANSAS
    LOUISIANA]

gives

TEXAS

and

PRINT BUTFIRST [TEXAS OKLAHOMA ARKANSAS
    LOUISIANA]

gives the list [OKLAHOMA ARKANSAS LOUISIANA]

The sub-programs in LOGO are known as procedures. A procedure for drawing a square can be defined by:

TO SQUARE
PENDOWN
REPEAT 4[FORWARD 100 RIGHT 90]
END

Once this is defined, a square can be drawn simply by issuing the command SQUARE in the same style as LOGO's own commands are issued. In this way the definition of procedures can be seen as a way of extending the language to suit the user. A more general way of defining a procedure to draw a square that can produce one of any size is:

TO SQUARE1 :SIDE
PENDOWN
REPEAT 4[FORWARD :SIDE RIGHT 90]
END

LOGO also supports recursion, that is, it has the ability that its procedures can call themselves. This provides a powerful technique for solving problems that can produce elegant solutions. A square can be drawn recursively with the procedure

```
TO SQUARE2 :SIDE
FORWARD :SIDE
RIGHT 90
SQUARE2 :SIDE
END
```

This illustrates that a procedure can call itself, although it is not a particularly good example of recursion as the procedure can never halt by itself. A better example, which does terminate, is the following, which uses the SQUARE1 procedure to produce a pattern of squares.

```
TO SQUAREPATTERN :SIDE
IF :SIDE > 100 [STOP]
SQUARE1 :SIDE
RIGHT 15
SQUAREPATTERN :SIDE+10
END
```

After making a list of procedure names, it is possible to write another procedure that will run the procedures in the list, either in order or at random. This is one step towards creating a microworld of your own.

Sprites are one of the important features of TI LOGO. They are handled in a way similar to that in Extended BASIC, with CARRY to give a sprite a shape, SETCOLOR to give it a colour, SETHEADING to fix its heading and, most importantly, SETSPEED to start it moving at a given speed along its heading.

TI LOGO, which is available as a plug-in module, also has sound and music capabilities.

Appendix 1
The ASCII Code

The TI99/4A uses the American Standard Code for Information Interchange (more commonly known as the ASCII code) as the code with which its standard characters are represented. The following table gives these characters and their codes.

ASCII Code	Character	ASCII Code	Character	ASCII Code	Character
32	(space)	65	A	97	A
33	! (exclamation point)	66	B	98	B
34	" (quote)	67	C	99	C
35	# (number or pound sign)	68	D	100	D
36	$ (dollar)	69	E	101	E
37	% (percent)	70	F	102	F
38	& (ampersand)	71	G	103	G
39	' (apostrophe)	72	H	104	H
40	((open parenthesis)	73	I	105	I
41	) (close parenthesis)	74	J	106	J
42	* (asterisk)	75	K	107	K
43	+ (plus)	76	L	108	L
44	, (comma)	77	M	109	M
45	− (minus)	78	N	110	N
46	. (period)	79	O	111	O
47	/ (slant)	80	P	112	P
48	0	81	Q	113	Q
49	1	82	R	114	R
50	2	83	S	115	S
51	3	84	T	116	T
52	4	85	U	117	U
53	5	86	V	118	V
54	6	87	W	119	W

55 7	88 X	120 X
56 8	89 Y	121 Y
57 9	90 Z	122 Z
58 : (colon)	91 [(open bracket)	123 { (left brace)
59 ; (semicolon)	92 \ (reverse slant)	124 :
60 < (less than)	93] (close bracket)	125 } (right brace)
61 = (equals)	94 ^ (exponentation)	126 ~ (tilde)
62 > (greater than)	95 _ (line)	127 DEL (appears on
63 ? (question mark)	96 ` (grave)	screen as a blank.)
64 @ (at sign)		

The codes are divided into sets for use with colour graphics created in programs using CALL COLOR as follows:

Set number	Character codes
1	32–39
2	40–47
3	48–55
4	56–63
5	64–71
6	72–79
7	80–87
8	88–95
9	96–103
10	104–111
11	112–119
12	120–127
13	128–135
14	136–143
15	144–151
16	152–159

Appendix 2
Binary And Hexadecimal Notation

In the binary number system there are only the two digits, 0 and 1, and all numbers are made up from them. Thus, a typical four digit number is 1101. In such a number, the least significant digit is, by convention, on the right and the most significant on the left. In fact, the position of each digit has a weighting factor associated with it to indicate its importance, and the weighting factors are, from right to left, 1, 2, 4, 8 and so on when a number has more than four digits. In fact, for binary numbers, the weighting factors are powers of two and can be written as 2^0, 2^1, 2^2, 2^3 and so on. Thus:

$$1101 = 1 \times 2^3 + 1 \times 2^2 + 0 \times 2^1 + 1 \times 2^0$$
$$= 8 + 4 + 1$$
$$= 13 \text{ on the decimal scale}$$

The base for hexadecimal numbers is sixteen, so that there are sixteen digits in this number system. They are represented by the numbers 0 to 9 and the letters A, B, C, D, E and F. Also, the weighting factors for the positional notation are powers of sixteen. Thus the hexadecimal number 27A2 is:

$$27A2 = 2 \times 16^3 + 7 \times 16^2 + 10 \times 16^1 + 2 \times 16^0$$
$$= 8192 + 1792 + 160 + 2$$
$$= 10146 \text{ in decimal}$$

Writing down the binary and hexadecimal numbers for counting from 0 to 15 (in decimal) we can see how to convert binary numbers to hexadecimal form and vice versa. The counting numbers are:

Decimal	Binary	Hexadecimal
0	0000	0
1	0001	1
2	0010	2

3	0011	3
4	0100	4
5	0101	5
6	0110	6
7	0111	7
8	1000	8
9	1001	9
10	1010	A
11	1011	B
12	1100	C
13	1101	D
14	1110	E
15	1111	F

From this, we can see that a group of four binary digits corresponds to one hexadecimal digit. Thus, a binary number can be converted to hexadecimal by dividing it into groups of four digits starting at the right and adding any leading zeros at the left as necessary, and then replacing each group by the equivalent hexadecimal digit. A hexadecimal number is converted to binary by replacing each digit with the equivalent group of four binary digits.

Appendix 3
Logic And Logical Expressions

The subject known as logic is one of the oldest branches of learning. It concerns propositions, which have the property that they are either true or false: there is no other possibility. Thus, a proposition can be used as a decision–rule for determining the membership of a set. The proposition 'X is a personal computer' is true for any X that *is* a personal computer, but is false for all others, and so can be used to generate the set of all personal computers. The fundamental concerns of logic are propositions and the ways in which they can be manipulated. As an example, the two propositions 'the TI99/4A is a personal computer' and 'the TI99/4A has colour graphics' can be combined into the single proposition 'the TI99/4A is a personal computer AND the TI99/4A has colour graphics' which is true since both its component propositions are true. Again, we can combine the two propositions 'Dallas is a coastal town' and 'Dallas is in Texas' to give 'Dallas is a coastal town OR Dallas is in Texas' which is also true despite the fact that its first component is false.

Our concern is with formal logic in which we study the form and combination of propositions without regard to their meaning and content. In this way, using 0 to represent false and 1 for true, the effects of the operators OR and AND can be represented by truth tables as in Chapter 3. The other common logical operators, which are provided in Extended TI BASIC are NOT and XOR. Their truth tables are:

A	NOT A
0	1
1	0

A	B	A XOR B
0	0	0
0	1	1
1	0	1
1	1	0

A logical expression is an arrangement of truth values, variables that have been assigned truth values and logical operators. When evaluated it will provide a value of 0 or 1, since as a combination of propositions, it is itself a proposition and must be true or false.

Just as in arithmetic expressions, the arithmetic operators have an order of precedence with, for example, multiplication done before addition, so there is an order of precedence for the logical operators. It is, from the most to the least importance, NOT, XOR, AND and OR. This order may be modified by using brackets. A logical expression is evaluated, therefore, by taking the operators in their correct order, applying them to their inputs to produce an output, as indicated by the truth tables, and continuing until the entire expression is dealt with.

The following example shows how a particular logical expression is handled:

        1 OR 0 AND NOT 1
        1 OR 0 AND 0
        1 OR 0
        1

Appendix 4
Notes And Further Reading

Chapter 1. Any amplification of the material of this chapter that the reader may require can be obtained from the User's Reference Guide.

Chapter 2. Information specific to the machine must be obtained, again, from the User's Reference Guide. A good deal of relevant information on graphics, and many ideas for graphics programs, can be found in *Programming With Graphics* by Garry Marshall, Granada, 1983. *BBC Micro Graphics And Sound* by Steve Money, Granada, 1983, is a source of useful ideas on graphics and sound that can be converted for the TI99/4A.

Chapter 3. The best way to develop a feel for the effectiveness of screen displays is probably to run a number of programs and to examine critically the displays they produce. The methods used to create the particularly effective ones can then be noted.

Chapter 4. The classic text on the systematic development of programs is *Structured Programming* by Dahl, Dijkstra and Hoare, Academic Press, 1972.

Chapter 5. A fruitful source of geometrical patterns is *Mathematical Models* by Cundy and Rollett, Oxford University Press, 1961. It contains three-dimensional patterns as well as two-dimensional ones. My source for Islamic patterns is *Pattern In Islamic Art* by D. Wade, Studio Vista, 1976. Many other patterns can be found in *Patterns In Nature* by P. S. Stevens, Penguin books, 1974.

The puzzle is based on 'Hungarian squares' which was devised by Stephen Shaw and published in *Computer and Video Games*, October 1982, pages 56–7. He also published 'Hungarian hex' in the same magazine in December 1982, pages 52–3.

Chapter 6. There are many books that contain listings of games for a particular microcomputer. The listings can be adapted readily for the TI99/4A, particularly if the books contain explanations of how the programs work.

Chapter 7. More information on writing and using databases can be found in *Databases For Fun And Profit* by Nigel Freestone, Granada, 1983.

Chapter 8. Another treatment of simulation can be found in *Computer Languages And Their Uses* by Garry Marshall, Granada, 1983.

Glossary

Animation: the creation of moving images.

Array: a set of variables which can be used in the same way as ordinary variables, but with the added convenience that they include a bracketed index. This makes arrays particularly suited for use with FOR ... NEXT loops.

ASCII code: American Standard Code for Information Interchange. A binary code used to represent characters numerically within the computer.

Assignment: A BASIC statement with which a number or a string of characters can be assigned to a variable to be stored under the name of the variable in the memory of the computer.

Background colour: the colour that is assigned to the background of a character when it is displayed on the screen.

BASIC: Beginner's All-purpose Symbolic Instruction Code. The high-level programming language that is used by almost all personal computers.

Binary: the number system with base two that uses only the digits 0 and 1.

Binary digit (bit): the digits of the binary number system, usually represented by 0 and 1.

Break point: a program line at which program execution halts to allow debugging and the examination of variables.

Byte: a group of eight binary digits.

Cassette: standard audio cassettes are used as the magnetic storage medium for the permanent storage of programs and data.

Character: any symbol that can be represented in the computer and displayed on its screen, including letters, numbers and graphics characters.

Character description: The special description used to define a new character. It consists of a string of hexadecimal digits. The way that it is arrived at is illustrated in Figure 2.5.

Character set: one of the sets into which the characters are divided for the allocation of their foreground and background colours by CALL COLOR.

Character string: a string of characters enclosed in quotation marks that can be displayed, stored or manipulated.

CLEAR key: this key is used to halt the execution of a program.

Code: an assignment of numbers to the characters by which they can be represented in the computer.

Colour graphics: coloured pictures and images created and displayed by the computer.

Command: a command to the computer that is obeyed as soon as it is issued. Examples of commands are RUN and LIST.

Conditional statement: The BASIC statement involving IF... THEN...ELSE that allows decisions to be made by a program.

Cursor: a flashing marker that shows where the next character to be displayed on the screen will be placed.

Data: numbers or characters that comprise the input to, or the output of, a program.

Database: an organised collection of data from which items of data can be retrieved in a variety of ways to suit the user.

Debugging: correcting the errors ('bugs') in a program.

Disk: a flexible plastic disk coated with a magnetic material. It is used to store data and programs by recording them magnetically on its surface. Also known as a floppy disk.

Dot matrix: the array of eight rows each containing eight dots that is used to display a character by turning some of the dots 'on' and leaving others 'off'.

EDIT: the command for editing a program line that permits characters in the line to be altered or deleted.

ENTER key: pressing the ENTER key at the end of a line causes the line to be sent to the computer to be dealt with, for example, a command is then obeyed and a program line is stored.

Expression: an arrangement of variables, values and operators that can be evaluated to provide a value.

Field: a sub-division of a record.

File: a collection of records treated as a single entity that can be stored on cassette or disk.

Flowchart: a diagram representing in stylised form the steps of a computer program.

Foreground colour: the colour that is assigned to the foreground of a character when it is displayed on the screen.

Graphics: pictures and images created and displayed by the computer.

Graphics character: a special character designed to form part of a picture or image, and defined with CALL CHAR.

Hexadecimal: the base sixteen number system having digits represented by 0 to 9 and A to F.

Information: the meaning attached to data, although also used to refer to the data itself.

Initialisation: the initial assignment of values to the variables in a program.

Input: the data entered for a program to process.

Interactive: The user can supply input to an interactive program while it is running, as opposed to having to halt it to do so.

Internal form: items stored in the computer's internal form are represented by binary numbers. They are, therefore, in a form that makes them suitable for the computer to handle, but unsuitable for display.

Joystick: a device for providing input that is used by many games programs. It is similar to the joystick of an aircraft.

Kilobyte: the unit for measurement of memory size. It equals 2^{10} or 1024 bytes, and is usually abbreviated as K.

Length (of a string): the number of characters in a string.

Line number: the number associated with a program line or statement. It is used to determine the position of a line in a program.

LIST: the command that causes the program currently stored in the computer to be displayed.

List processing: a style of computing in which data is placed in lists. Computer languages for list processing have special features for handling lists.

Logic: the manipulation of binary digits (representing the truth values true and false) using logical operators such as OR and AND.

Logical expression: an expression consisting of logical values, variables and operators.

Logical operators: operators for manipulating binary digits or truth values.

LOGO: a high-level computer language with facilities for controlling a turtle and for list processing.

Loop: a sequence of statements to be executed repeatedly. One can be constructed by surrounding the sequence with FOR and NEXT statements

Machine code: a language understood directly by a microprocessor with no need for translation.

Master selection list: the display showing the items that the user may select for the computer to run.

Master title screen: the initial display produced by the computer when it is switched on, and which is also displayed after the QUIT key is pressed.

Memory: the computer's memory consists of read only memory (ROM) in which information is stored permanently, e.g. for BASIC, and random access memory (RAM) in which the user's program and data are stored, but only for as long as the computer remains switched on.

Microworld: a restricted world that can be created with LOGO, and used as a vehicle for learning when experimented with or explored.

Noise: random sounds that can only be characterised statistically.

Output: the output, typically results, that are displayed or stored by a program.

Program: a sequence of statements. When a computer runs a program, it executes each statement in succession. It can carry out a task by running a program that gives it detailed instructions for doing so.

Program development: the process of designing and writing a program.

Program structure: the arrangement of the parts of a program.

Prompt: a character displayed or a noise produced by the computer to indicate that it expects a response.

Random number: an unpredictable number between zero and one that is generated using RND.

Record: a collection of fields that represents all the aspects of interest for some type of item.

REMark: a statement starting with REM that is used to document a program.

Repetition: the repeated execution of a statement or sequence of statements, usually realised by surrounding them with FOR and NEXT statements.

Reserved word: a special word that forms part of the BASIC language and therefore may not be used as a variable name.

RUN: the command for executing the program that is currently stored in the computer.

Screen position: The screen is divided into 24 rows and 32 columns. A screen position is identified by giving its row and column.

Scrolling: since a new line is always displayed at the bottom of the screen, the whole screen moves up by one line (scrolls up) before the line is printed to provide a clear bottom line for it, but losing the previous top line at the same time.

Separator: one of the special characters for separating the items in DISPLAY and PRINT statements.

Simulation: a program that imitates or catches the essence of a real or a proposed system.

Sprite: a graphics character that has the extra attribute of movement.

Statement: a program line consisting of a number followed by a command.

String: a string, or sequence, of characters enclosed in quotation marks.

Structured programming: the process of developing a program with a good, clear structure.

Subroutine: a self-contained sub-program that can be called from a main program to perform a task that it may require several times.

Task: a job for which a program is to be written.

Text: a display composed of words.

TI BASIC: the version of BASIC supplied with the computer.

Tile: a graphics character.

Tone: a note with a definite pitch. Its waveform is a sine wave.

Top-down design: a method of structured programming that involves continuously refining tasks into sub-tasks, until sub-tasks are arrived at that are simple to program.

Trace: a trace of the order in which program lines are executed when a program is run. Rather than TRACE some systems use the word TRON.

Truth table: a table showing the output produced by a logical operator for each of its possible inputs.

Turtle: a wheeled mechanical device (floor turtle) or a shape on the screen (screen turtle) that can be controlled by commands from LOGO.

Variable: that to which a value can be assigned for storage, and the name of which can be used to refer to the stored value.

Index